FBI ANTI-PIRACY WARNING

The unauthorized reproduction or distribution of this copyrighted work is illegal. Criminal copyright infringement, including infringement without monetary gain, is investigated by the FBI and is punishable by up to 5 years in federal prison and a fine of $250,000.

Copyright Notice

No part of this publication or creative content may be reproduced, distributed, used or transmitted in any form or by any means, including photocopying, recording, or other electronic or mechanical methods, without the prior written permission of the author, except in the case of brief quotations embodied in reviews and certain other noncommercial uses permitted by copyright law.

Disclaimer Notice

No part of this book is intended to replace medical, legal, or professional mental help related to any possible topic, subject, issue, or element within this book. Although the author and publisher have made every effort to ensure that the information in this book was correct at press time, the author and publisher do not assume and hereby disclaim any liability to any party for any loss, damage or disruption caused by error, omissions, or analysis, whether such errors result from negligence, accident, or any other cause. Any resemblance to actual persons, living or dead, or actual events is purely coincidental.

PUBLISHER:

THE AI ORGANIZATON

4275 EXECUTIVE SQUARE STE 200, LA JOLLA, CA, 92037

ISBN Paperback Edition: **978-1-953059-24-6**

About the Author

Director Parsa has advised CIA directors, POTUS, other members of the intelligence community at the highest levels on AI, UFOs, China, human trafficking and matters of national security.

Cyrus personally was shown 100s of files, images of aliens and their ships in the year 2003 by the main person leading the reverse engineering on alien crafts. Cyrus also witnessed while in the mountains of China multiple UFO flybys at night and has come in contact with UFOs on multiple occasions.

He has a B.S. in International Security, Master's in Homeland Security, lived with fighting monks in China, and has trained in martial meditative arts for over 20 years.

Cyrus is an avid motorcycle rider, loves humanity & works to safeguard its future. Cyrus has been featured on multiple UFO Alien podcasts, most notably on the Nationally Syndicate Show with George Noory, Coast to Coast, a total of 5 times.

Currently Cyrus is shooting a movie called AI WARS: Alien Invasion. Support it at Godstudios.com. His movie and comic is about a long term secret invasion plot by aliens to replace the human race at every level powered by AI, leading to AI WARS, involving hypersonic nuclear weapons.

Cyrus also predicted, detected and warned to all major media and intelligence community leaders in the fall of 2019 of a bioweapon coming from China with great effort to save your lives, freedoms and prevent global unrest/wars.

Cyrus used his third eye AKA Pineal Gland, remote viewing to detect Covid 19, and then used his military and intelligence assets to verify the lab in China.

Many Presidents, heads of Intelligence agencies, global tech billionaires, media moguls, admirals and Generals, and the leaders of China's Government not only hid Cyrus's 2019 virus and force mandate warnings, but they conspired to hide his story by aligning with evil forces unknowingly, hurting You, your families, the world and themselves.

Synopsis

How was the first STD created? Do you carry other people's emotions, trauma and health issues when you sleep around? How does the male sperm DNA and other male organisms penetrate and stay in the female brain?

How are you manipulated? Who is a real friend? What is the Virginity Code? How does cannabis AKA Weed/ Marijuana and alcohol, AI and your social media add risks to you and your loved ones being trafficked, raped, catching an STD or being in a bad relationship with unhappiness?

Learn how to protect your wife, husband, daughter, son, brother, friend from betrayal, adultery, bad relationships, alcoholism, drug addiction, and unhappiness from casual sex and picking the wrong partner in your life. This is an additional book continuation from my research and 2019 publication of the book Raped via Bio-Digital Social Programming. More so, learn about the secrets of the Virginity Code and your energy field.

I am Cyrus Parsa, Founder of the AI Organization and God Studios. I used AI, Lidar, facial, voice, gaze, posture, skeleton, organ and other secret tools to see through the human body, its cells and its relation to Sex to verify all my findings that I have seen through my Pineal Gland, AKA

Third Eye, the past 24 years.

I single handedly warned of the Bioweapon lab from China starting in June 2019 in writing, and orally to world leaders, Presidents, CIA Directors, Secret Service and all major media. I warned that it would enslave the world, kill lots of people, riots, loss of freedoms, famines mandated vaccines with Nanotech, all leading to global wars with hypersonic missiles.

I used my intel groups to verify what I saw with my third eye and remote viewing, and it was all accurate and will be verified because it's all in writing, including federal documents dated 2019 Dec and Feb 2020 as well as my books and intelligence reports in 2019. I was also on over 300 podcasts, including UFO ones with George Noory a total of 6 times. I managed to get the UFO files declassed with my film documentary AI The Plan to Invade Humanity.

Everything I did, was in an attempt to save the lives and freedoms of you, your families, your friends, and your loved ones. I took no money, other than a little amount from my book sales and sacrificed greatly. However, major owners of media outlets wrote global notices in their attempt to hide my story and warnings due to their ignorance in their collusion with podcasters and very selfish people who caused you to suffer during the lockdowns more than you would have if my story was given global attention by all major media and if I was supported by you, the reader.

This book, Virginity Code for the first time reveals secret things related to sex and your energy field. I hope it is well received and for you to support the Virginity Code by getting copies and supporting me financially so I can make the movie AI WARS to eliminate world tensions. Purposely I wrote this book in a way to be short, with main points to give you the big picture.

My credibility is a B.S in International Security, Masters in Homeland Security, PhD. Education, 24 years of strengthening myself through an ancient meditation and spiritual practice system which provided me with enhanced energy, wisdom, and abilities, plus 20 years of investigations, research and discoveries made together with a network of hundreds of people worldwide, and the tireless laboring and sacrifices made especial during the pandemic, working on your behalf, notifying the world to prevent the global dangers that are upon humanity..

VIRGINITY CODE

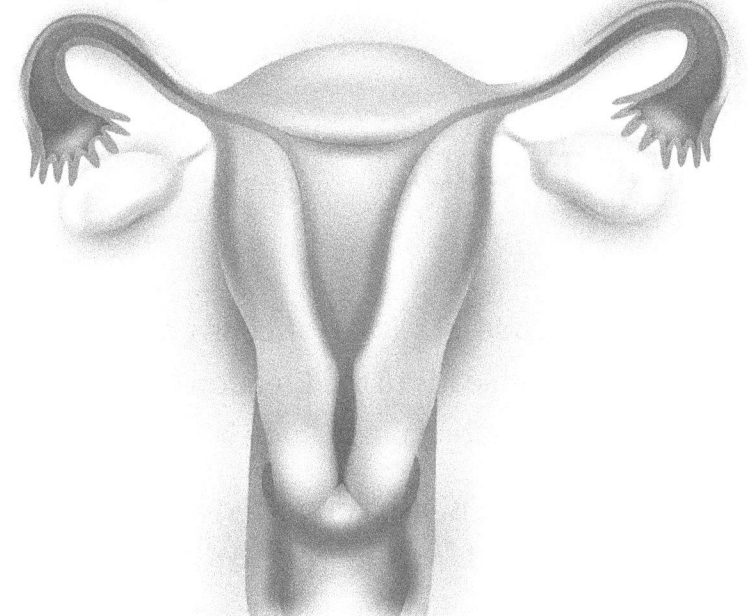

SEX CODES FOR A HEALTHY MIND, BODY AND SPIRIT

CYRUS A. PARSA
THE AI ORGANIZATION

VIRGINITY CODE

Sex Codes for a Healthy Mind, Body and Spirit

INTRODUCTION

VIRGINITY CODE

The Virginity code is a layer of codes and programs in the human body that leads to the Creation Code and connects to the Universal Cheating Curse Code if violated.

The Virginity Code is also connected in between the human body, brain, mind and spirit that leads to the human Consciousness, Subconsciousness and Unconsciousness.

You can think of it as a portal in between worlds within the universe of the human body at the micro levels as well as the macro levels. For a woman, you see a vagina, uterus, etc., however, at the micro-level you see a tremendous organism designed to produce and carry life as well a dimension as big as a universe with meaning.

The Virginity Code is not simply related to sex and virginity, rather the inner workings of the human body leading to lifespan, Destiny, health, fitness, happiness purpose, longevity, birth, law, truth, purity and enlightenment.

The Creation Code

The Creation code is a built-in code that connects to the virginity code. Within the creation code exists loyalty, love, respect, spirituality, nobleness, hygiene, monogamy, and faithfulness, and it is all governed by the Creation Law built into the human body as a code. It is designed to promote and protect the virginity code.

If the creation code is violated, broken by unfaithfulness, or sleeping around, the creation code attacks the virginity code producing the universal cheating curse code.

Syphilis, Chlamydia, HP1, HIV, Gonorrhea, and a myriad of sexual and human microorganisms physically are created and enter the human hosts, as well as a bio-electric karmic field that produces depression, emotional instability, bad health.

Next, Universal Cheating Curse Code alters the brain chemistry of the human host towards unhappiness and a void of spiritual emptiness.

Universal Cheating Curse Code

If you cheat on a wife, husband, boyfriend, girlfriend, spouse, the universe will curse you. The code is written in your DNA, computed by your brain to detect if you cheat and determines the code of cheating as a wrongful act against your very nature and the universal code.

By committing the act of adultery, or cheating, your body will automatically create depression for you, and illnesses down the line.

The DNA instructs this very exact thing to happen because in the DNA exists the Virginity Code that links to the Creation Code. It affects each person differently.

From depression, and even terminal illnesses like heart disease, cancer as the Sexual transmitted diseases and microorganisms spread through the human body. etc.

Chapter 1

Male Sperm DNA in Female Brain

Through multiple AI and technological apparatus, I discovered that through sex, particularly the ejaculation of the male sperm into the women, the man's DNA, sex micro bacteria, Dormant STDs and Sperm DNA is transferred over to the new host, the female, for life.

This is also true in the case of multiple partners for the women. If she has had 10 males, she has had sexual contact with, she will have the DNA, micro sex bacteria and other dormant parasitical bacteria living inside of her that is invisible to the human eye.

The living micro sex bacteria and dormant parasitical bacteria from the males inside the women will be mutating and reaching her brain in conjunction with the other males DNA.

The multiple DNA and bacteria of men living inside of the women will create a biochemistry mess, emotional instability, trauma, dormant sexual disease, reduced immune system in the long run, and a potential spiritual and mental deficiency for life.

Because of the parasitical nature of the different male's sperm and micro bacteria fighting each other for dominance, the multiple foreign bacteria living inside the women will cause instability and dysfunction to her biochemistry in the long run.

You may say, well, the sperm dies within 5 days or so if a woman is not impregnated. Yes, but not the genetic information of the DNA carried over by the micro bacteria transferred from the male's sperm, penis, saliva, and sweat poisons of the human body.

At some point, the sperm and other male bacteria and DNA is mutated and transferred over to the female brain and can be found at the point of dissection.

It is not only the experiences that you have that put imprints into your brain, rather the micro bacteria from the multiple sex partners a female carries.

This is also true for the male's brain, but rather only from her micro-bacteria and not a reproductive element found in men such as sperm.

Is it true you can find the male sperm DNA of each person a woman has had sex within her brain upon dissection? If so, how does it relate to the Virginity Code?

There are scientific studies done that claim and prove to varying degrees that human sperms DNA data is stored in the female brain and DNA through sex. First, let's discuss this from an ancient perspective.

In ancient times, it was said that a man's essence is physically and spiritually passed down into a woman not only to create life, but to create a union between the two bodies.

You will find this in Zoroastrian, Mithraism and Catholic writing as well as Jewish writings. It is also stated in Sufi mystical ways as well as in Indian literature.

With Aristotle of Greece, and the idea of telegony, it was said that individuals can inherit traits not only from their father, rather the males the women previous had slept with.

In Tantrism sex, it was said in ancient times that the energetic materials that make up life can be transferred from a male to a female and from a female to a man, to alter each person's DNA and energies found in the human body in order to transform the body.

In Falun Dafa Qi Gong rooted in Taoist and Buddhist Alchemy, it goes even further by teaching that an individual can use his or her vital essence that makes up their sperm or eggs to create a type of fusion in their body to transform not just their cells, rather their spirit housed in their physical body. Sort of like a glorified body, but in the mortal plane.

Parasitical Sperm Control of Women

The micro bacterial particles inside the sperm of a man does to varying degrees take control or influence over the women's thoughts, emotions and brain not just during pregnancy, but simply by exchanging ones DNA through sex as the sperm enters the women.

First, the sperm is designed to impregnate the women with his DNA, and two, to alter her thoughts through her reproductive system.

However, there is an additional component which I call the parasitical sperm control of a women. The parasitical sperm design in a male system is in part meant to ensure the women is under the control of a man to guarantee faithfulness above her sexual urges and outside societal influence during the pregnancy and beyond.

If pregnancy fails, a man's sperm still acts in a parasitic way lodging itself inside a women's DNA in order to give her a memory, a feeling or something to come back to for the man and women. It is sort of like how an animal marks its territory in a place by taking a piss.

In fact, some animals can sense if their mate has been with another, in the past. Their sense of smell is remarkable and can sense things even if from the past.

"Hutchinson Center study finds male DNA in women's brains"

Research in Dr. Lee Nelson's lab showed high frequency of male microchimerism in the female brain, found it to impact a woman's risk of developing some types of cancer and autoimmune disease.

Albeit it was females who were pregnant prior to death, I argue, discovered and have known for some time that micro-bacteria from the male sperm and DNA does enter the female in multiple ways and does not require pregnancy to enter the woman's brain. This will be discussed as the book, Virginity Code, progresses.

Electrical Sex Imprints-Female Brain

Whatever you see, hear and do leaves an electrical imprint into your brain and bioelectrical human field as an experience or memory. Even if you develop Alzheimer's, the memories can still be extracted from the brain, digital mind or your energy field.

Pain, suffering, emotional experiences as well as tragic and toxic experiences are all stored in the human brain within digital layers, and even carried in your cells, blood, and other components of your body and energy field.

Sexual activity, with multiple partners throughout time, is stored in the human brain, blood, cells and other areas of the human body as real messages comprised of energy, electrical signals and memory.

Most of these memories are in your subconscious mind and unconscious mind and can be accessed by your conscious mind if you try to think about it, which is not a great idea for the most part.

Because those electrical impulses are real energy and carry negative qualities, if you try to think about them, it will bring them over to your conscious mind, weighing on your health, mind and spirit. Thus, affecting your daily life and health with a heavy spirit.

In fact, the electrical impulses and energies from your previous sexual partners is already negatively impacting you at the subconscious and unconscious level, carrying depression and sadness you cannot really pinpoint or see at the conscious levels in energetic form housed inside your energy field composed of bio-electrical materials.

The electrical impulses from each person the females have sexual relations with carries a different frequency and wavelength unique to that man's health, character, thoughts, state of mind, vice, virtue, amount of black toxic karmic energy field, "Sin" and spiritually obtained level, if any.

The more sexual partners a female takes in, the more emotional garbage, and energetic material made up of their sex partners thoughts, mind, character, health, sickness and spiritual illnesses, they absorb.

This is the same and true for the man. The more sexual partners and bio-electrical data and energy you take in from females, the more you injure and ruin yourself.

Each person is like a program with a certain amount of positive and negative qualities. And these traits can be decoded not only from a person's genes, and actions, but with the right configuration of machines and other apparatus from the energy and electrical signals residing in their brains, mind, energy field and spirits.

Electrical & Energetic SEX VIRUS

A virus can impede the functioning of the program in your phone, or computer. If you take in too much, it can shut parts of your computer down, if not all of it down.

Electrical and Energy SEX Virus's from people's energy fields exist and can be transferred into you by way of sexual contact and sexual intercourse similar to how a virus enters a computer or smart phone through frequencies you do not see.

Yes, you not only have to worry about Sexually Transmitted Diseases in a traditional sense affecting your skin and organs, but you also have to worry about electrical and energetic sexual transmitted diseases via the mind, body, energy field and spirit that make up your bioelectrical field.

The more negative messages, and bioelectrical fields your partners carry in their bodies and minds, the more negative bioelectrical messages and electrical impulses you take in, infecting your health, mind and spirit.

This is because the human body is also made out of electricity and a life-force the Persians called Magi, or later called by the Europeans Magic, the Indians Prana, the Chinese Qi or Chi and we call Energy or bio-electrical energy field.

If your partner carries sadness, selfishness, ego, pride, jealousy, deception, fear, and various vice and health issues that are reinforced by his or her state of mind, your sexual activity with them is exposing you at the bio-electrical level to their garbage housed in their bio-electrical energy fields.

Add 10 sexual partners in your life, you have been exposed to 10 of their bio-electric energy fields and their garbage that resides in their energy fields, including their physical, mental and spiritual sicknesses.

Add the number of times you have had sexual intercourse or activity, and duration of sexual contact, you increase the exposure and how much bio-electrical disease you carry in your energy field, mind and spirit or consciousness.

Bio-Electrical Sexual Transmitted Diseases

You may think you are avoiding a sexually transmitted disease by wearing a condom, not kissing and making minimal skin contact, but you are in essence exchanging your bio-electrical fields and making bio electrical sexual contacts with your partner.

You are obtaining a Bio-Electrical Sexually Transmitted disease that carries a mass of energy from your partners bio-electrical energy field composed of their state of mind, sadness, depression, and many bad characteristics that are made up of black energetic karma.

This black energetic karma, later in life creates real concrete sickness for them and for you if you take too much of it into your body and energy field.

What does this mean? This means, not only are you obtaining bio-electrical sexually transmitted diseases, but bit by bit you are obtaining their bio-electric karma that creates their lives sadness, depression and even their destiny.

Think about what I have revealed here and how important this secret is to the intelligent person who will understand it and not dismiss it as if they were a buffoon?

Think about what you are risking when you are sleeping around? It is not only an STD, but a black energetic karma that can affect your health, mind, emotions, spirit, and even your destiny in a negative way.

You are getting your partner or multiple partners negative, or in religious terms sinful and karmic energies through sexual contact.

And even energy that makes up their mind, emotions, mental state, and character that is influencing you, and partially infecting and replacing your own emotions, mental state and character.

Why? Because energy is made up of electrical and bio-electrical particles at the molecular level and atomic and beyond. And energy can mutate and multiply just like a physical virus at the cellular level.

We are bioelectrical beings like a computer with hardware and software. Hence, your software is the energy in your body and what is comprised of your mind and spirit and bio-electrical field as well as your life-force, Qi.

Your hardware would be your organs, bones, cells, etc. However, if you look deeper, you will see the human body is much more sophisticated than a computer.

Then you will realize your organs, and cells, albeit physical, have bio-electrical energy running through them, which can be deemed also as your software as well. Because your life-force runs through them and is housed inside your organs.

Sexual Animality VS Loving Sexuality

Sexuality comes with either animality or a loving sexuality. Animality is strictly one of carnal desire and actions, much like how animals partake in during sex. One without respect or love.

On the other hand, those with a higher consciousness, more evolved or filled with spiritual love, would only partake in intimacy when there is a sense of respect, love, loyalty and faithful harmony with one partner with hopes of a long-term relationship. This falls more in line with the Virginity Code. I argue that it exists in the DNA and Software of the human body.

Sometimes it is a mix of the two, animality and loving sexuality. Yet true loving intimacy in a relationship would not contain animality during intimacy and be one of pure monogamy like the Swans you see that mate for life.

Beast Nature Vs Soul Nature

A beast in the wild will rape, manipulate, have many sexual partners and see the sexual partner as an object. There are people who fall under this radar of beast nature by using the label of "Open Relationship" to get away with cheating or the fact that they can't love or have fallen into this trap of despair.

For example, there are females or males who use the title of open relationships to coerce their partners, wives or husbands to accept their infidelity by emotionally wearing down their partners and making they dependent mentally and physically on the perceived fake love. More will be said about this under "Open Relationship."

Chapter 2

The First Sexually Transmitted Disease

How did the first sexually transmitted disease come into creation?

According to modern scientists and Doctors you believe to be experts, the notion exists that someone already must have an STD in order to get an STD.

But, I argue an STD can be simply created between 3 or more people simply by promiscuity. Sleeping with more than one person and sharing saliva, sweat, DNA, Etc.

Moreover, within the human body exists a virginity code that produces a creation code that leads to a universal cheat curse code. These codes will be explained in depth later.

If you exchange a kiss with another person, then you or the other person kiss another and re-kiss each other some time in the future, you are exchanging not only your own bacteria, but the 3rd person's bacteria in between.

For example, if John kisses Jennifer, and Jeniffer kisses Jack, the saliva, bacteria from John is carried over to Jack through Jennifer.

This transference of bacteria will live inside Jennifer and Jack and carry back to John if they share a kiss again.

More troubling, if John's bacteria inside of Jennifer mutates with Jennifer, a new form of Bacteria is created, potentially into a strong form of STD to pass onto Jack.

If sex and bodily contact where sweat glands are touching are involved, various forms of sexually transmitted diseases can be created between the 3 hosts.

The sexually transmitted diseases created between the 3 persons can show up in one's lives months or years down the line in different forms of human illnesses that are emotional, mental, physical and spiritual.

Now, take into consideration that many people have had between 1-20 partners in the 21st century, a great deal of people are spreading a variety of sexuality transmitted diseases and or strains of bacteria that are infecting everyone who comes into contact with them unknowingly affecting their physical and mental health.

These bacteria and STDs living inside the human hosts may show or develop into something that modern science recognizes as an illness or sexually transmitted disease, as the persons immune system breaks down months, years or in some cases, a couple decades down the line.

In essence, having sex with more than one person, regardless of if they have any STDs, can form a sexually transmitted disease simply by sharing microorganisms on the skin, sweat glands, or saliva.

The invisible will form something that is visible, a bigger organism which we call a sexually transmitted disease or immune dysfunction of the bodily organs.

Let me give you a sneak peek at a bigger secret that you will read about further in the virginity code with regard to the invisible forming into the visible.

The bio-electrical diseases, and bio-electrical fields or energy fields inside the human bodies of your partners can aid or create micro-organisms or STDs inside of your body or your sex partners in casual sex, open relationships or when you conduct yourself with promiscuity.

At the microscopic molecular levels and even the atomic layers, there is a virginity code built in as well. And the bioelectrical fields that exist at the micro levels in your molecules can and at some points do instruct and create STDs at the cellular level for humans that appear or felt at some point in a person's life.

It's kind of like magic or a horrible disease for human beings. Let's look at sexually transmitted diseases in the next sections from a different perspective in addition to your modern knowledge of STDs.

Sexual Transmitted Disease

Sexually transmitted diseases are not limited to the physical ones known by modern machines such as Gonorrhea, Chlamydia, HP1, HP2, Herpes, HIV, Hepatitis, and the like.

No, as outlined in this book, there is DNA transfer, and micro bacteria that can act or mutate into becoming a disease as well as unseen bioelectrical elements.

More so, within the Virginity Code of the huma body, emotional trauma, stress, sadness, depression, reduced immunity, organ disfunction, mental instability, and an injured spirit, all can be considered or act like a sexually transmitted disease when you go against the virginity code in your body.

STD Persia-

Persians were known for inventing numerous products for hygiene as well as writing books on hygiene from multiple dynasties starting with Cyrus the Great almost 2600 hundred years ago.

They had similar court etiquette to the Chinese and valued monogamy greatly not simply because of love, nobleness, family, rather to prevent disease and keep clean.

Hence, hugging, touching, promiscuity or having multiple partners even in marriage, was seldom promoted, until the invasion from the Arabs and Mongols which brought sex slavery, 4 wives, and Sighe. Sighe, is an Islamic term that sanctions sex outside of marriage for 1 night or more based on contract mainly against the "Ajam".

Just like the Talmud book of the Jews has the word Goyum for non-Jews, the Arabs have the word Ajam for non-Arabs.

Both are derogatory and promoted racial and religious supremacy over other races, peoples and religions according to their texts or at the very least, according to historical practices against the Goyum and Ajam.

Now, if you look at Europe, especially the Romans and Greeks, you shall see many plagues and sexual diseases spread due to their promiscuous, casual lifestyles right before their empires were destroyed.

Some scholars and Persian stories state that the Persians became decadent and unhygienic sexually, just like the Romans did, and thus they lost their empires not simply because of war, rather they lost their virtue, and their mental stability was destroyed due to alcoholism and casual promiscuity, adding to their greed, pride and egos.

Do you find this phenomenon today in America and around the world? Greed, Pride, Egos, Jealousy, Alcoholism and casual promiscuity?

STD CHINA

In every dynasty, in particular the Tang Dynasty, China had protocols between men and women, and physical contact in general. Shaking hands and hugs did not exist due to hygiene and personal space.

You can see in court etiquette and martial arts practices, people were told prior to the 1940s to keep a distance, greet each other with hand signs as you would see by martial arts master's and so on.

In Ancient China, there was no such thing as hugs between friends or strangers, only close relatives or between a husband and wife, or a mother and child.

The practice of space and lack of touch was not only a religious, or cultural practice for the Chinese, it was a hygienic one meant to prevent disease, including STDs through kiss, hepatitis, and the plague and and so on.

ORAL SEX DISEASES

Microorganisms and bacteria from oral sex and kissing can lie dormant in the tongue, mouth and lips from previous partners.

When the immune system breaks down through the years or when more exposure to new partners is made, the microorganism and bacteria from previous oral sex and kissing within the tongue, lips and mouth can transform into cancer.

KISSING

Through a kiss, bacteria and disease can transfer reaching inside your organs with micro bacterial particles replicating and mutating inside of you.

All kinds of sexually transmitted diseases such Chlamydia, Gonorrhea, Herpes, Hp1, Hepatitis and a lot more can be transferred over.

For some, a kiss and the STD can simply lie dormant for months, years or even decades in the mouth until it mutates, as your immune system no longer can keep it at bay.

Throat Cancer

Through oral sex with multiple partners, or with 1 partner who has had oral sex with multiple partners, an STD can mutate and transform into throat cancer.

In fact, the code within the virginity code is triggered and begins to break down the immunity within the mouth through a long-term process after being exposed with sexually transmitted bacterial particles that can mutate to cancerous cells within the mouth and throat.

Tongue Cancer

Tongue cancer can be had from bacteria that lies dormant from kissing or oral sex within an individual who had come into contact sexually with a person that carries a mutated bacterial forming cancer formed by casual sex.

Heart Disease and STD

A sexually transmitted disease, or micro bacterial particles from another person can enter through kissing, oral, penetrated sex or through the sweat glands when touching during intimacy.

These microparticles and STDs can enter a person's heart in a mutated form causing long term heart disease or contribute to a heart attack through the bacteria penetrating the blood stream as it pumps back into the heart. Another reason not to sleep around and follow the Virginity Code in my view.

This is a silent killer that has been not only a secret but beyond the comprehension and understanding of modern doctors.

As they can only relate heart condition to smoking, eating habits and stress, rather sexual health and character as it was done in ancient times by sophisticated cultures.

Stroke and STD

STDs can not only injure your immunize system, nervous system, liver, kidney and so on, but they can weaken your Qi Flow as well as the functioning of your organs, causing mini strokes in your body after years of having the STD knowingly through tests or as it lies dormant inside of your body.

Dormant Saliva DNA

A person's saliva can carry HIV, sexually transmitted diseases, and even carry bacteria that can form other diseases with the interaction of your saliva through sexual contact.

More so, a person's mental and emotional states are not simply an energetic electrical substance, their positivity and negativity exist in one's bacteria and saliva, and can be transferred into you via a kiss, sex, and bodily contact via sweat.

Fungal Infection Sex

Micro bacteria from casual sex can interact with fungal bacteria you are exposed with to make the fungal infection more potent, or more likely to occur with new strains created from the partners foreign bacteria that has entered you.

Sepsis Sex

Sepsis can occur more readily if your immune system is affected, infected or weakened by STDs or different micro bacteria that have entered your blood stream from another person whom you have had sexual relations with or if you are unlucky enough, your partner is carrying it because she or he has recently cheated on you.

Hepatitis Through Sex

Many forms of Hepatitis exist, and some are dormant in a person's body undetected by tests or any exams. However, dormant Hepatitis can be transmitted to you through sharing cups, food, kissing, sex and oral sex.

In addition, through other forms of STDs and Micro Bacteria existing in your partners bodies, whether dormant or test positive diseases can intermingle with dormant hepatitis to create a stronger form of sexual diseases or hepatitis.

Another very important health reason to stay away from casual sex, multiple partners and consider the Virginity Code as outlined in this book.

Diabetes through Sex

When exchanging saliva, your DNA is also interacting with your sexual partner. If your partner has blood sugar issues, the elements that makes them unhealthy is in their blood stream, as well as in their saliva and sweat.

You can obtain the micro bacteria that is contributing to their blood sugar problems, and a couple decades later you may develop blood sugar issues, even though genetically and from a diet standpoint you would not have if you did not sleep around, in particular with that person.

Blood Pressure Issues

Sleeping around with multiple people will expose you with multiple different micro bacteria that your immune system, heart and kidneys will work hard to expel, causing your blood pressure to go up in the long run.

You may run into blood pressure issues not just from the micro bacteria, but the stress from the emotional trauma of going through so many relationships or casual sex partners.

IBS Issues

Peoples IBS issues can significantly worsen through sleeping around with multiple partners as they take in their micro bacteria through skin contact, oral, vaginal sex, kissing, sharing cups, food, as well as touching.

The more worry, stress a person takes from casual sex, or one relationship after another, the worse their IBS will become.

Crohn's Disease

Some people's IBS and stomach issues through the years turn into Crohn's disease which is generally not curable, a life-long illness and can be terminal for some.

Crohn's disease can develop more rapidly for individuals with preexisting conditions who engage in casual sex compromising their immune systems.

Sex on Medications, Humera Shots

You may have an illness that requires Humera shots, or different medications. By you sleeping around and getting other people's STDs or micro bacteria, you are exposing other bacteria and issues that may make your medications unresponsive, or not as affective, causing your illnesses to worsen unknowingly.

Hence, think about the Virginity Code and choose your partners wisely by considering how many partners they have had, whether they have STDs, their emotional state, their character, and if they have drug and alcohol addictions.

Lung Cancer Kissing

When you are kissing a person, that person's airborne bacteria is entering you and interacting with your lungs. If they carry long-covid, those micro-covid particles will enter your lungs.

If they carry bacteria in their mouth that does not harmonize with your bacteria, in the long term his or her bacteria can infect your lungs. In rare cases, it can even lead to lung cancer if a contagious form of bacteria enters you.

Gum Disease Kissing

When kissing, a person's gum health is partially compromised of the bacteria in their mouth and gums, as well as micro bacteria from previous sexual partners.

Their bacteria can at the micro-level infect your mouth and gums, and you may or will get the negative results from that infection years down the line.

Weakened Immune System Sex

Those with weakened immune systems should not engage in casual sex because they are a lot more susceptible to micro bacteria and catching STDs which would greatly weaken their immune systems and may cause organ failure.

Organ Failure Sex-Kidneys

Some people who sleep around introduce multiple different micro bacteria from their casual sex partners which attacks their organs.

In ancient Chinese medicine it is said that too much sex, especially masturbation will weaken and deplete your life-force from your kidneys.

In particular, if it is sex with multiple people, it could reduce your lifespan and or cause kidney failure later on.

Weakened Eyesight

Too much sex, and especially too much masturbation will weaken your eyesight because the energy in your kidneys is being depleted.

The kidneys regulate the source that gives the energy for your eyesight. This is very important and explained not only in Chinese medicine, but in Persian Culture rooted in their ancient medicine as well.

Sex, Kidneys, Masturbation, Hair loss

In Persian, Italian, and Chinese culture, those who lose a lot of hair did so because they are either genetically coded to lose it, through stress, bad diet and of course with some, through a great deal of sex and masturbation.

If you speak with some seasoned hair transplant doctors, they will tell you some of their patients complain of kidney pain after a hair transplant.

And that is because the kidneys are the power source that regulates hair growth in the hair if your hair loss is not genetic.

Those patients had weak kidneys, had their hair transplant operations and had side effects in their kidneys because of the overbearing pressure on their kidneys to provide nutrients to other areas in their scalp that have now had FUE or FUT transplantation from the donor areas.

So yes, in ancient Chinese and Persian medicine, Qi Gong and Meditation are very advanced and what they explained about thought, conduct, the life-force and your kidneys are real and I can personally attest to it from experience.

I have meditated for over 20 years, and can feel my blood flow, cells moving, neurons firing, multiple kinds of Qi and electricity moving in my body and how each organ works.

I have experienced 1000s of extra sensory perceptions through the years we do not even have names for. This means, I have a certain medical knowledge of the human body and medicine unmatched by any Doctor on the planet who got his or her degree from reading books and using machines.

I know and can sense how thoughts, what you eat, and every action a human does, affects the human organs and the human body, mind and spirit.

What I accomplished through my years of sometimes training 10-18 hours a day is very advanced.

Dormant Sexual Disease

Dormant sexually transmitted diseases can be comprised of chlamydia, gonorrhea, herpes, HIV, HP1, HP2, syphilis and a variety of other STDs that will form with micro bacteria your body carries after being in sexual contact with more than 1 person.

The dormant STD or Micro Bacteria could take 5, 10, 20 or even 30 years to break down your immune system and show up on a test.

However, during that process it may and often does affect your thoughts, biochemistry and ways of thinking as well as stress levels just like a stomach parasite would.

The micro bacteria and STDs are in fact at the micro level a life form, they are live bacteria with a program. What program do you say?

To multiply and invade other organisms and replace them with itself, the sexually transmitted disease or bacteria.

At any time, you can get in your system micro bacteria that is sexual in nature from sex, oral sex, kissing, a person's sweat glands, touch and even sharing drinks and food.

And these micro bacteria may be dormant for years unbeknownst to you affecting your organs, your health, mind and quality of life.

Hence, best not sleep around and practice great hygiene as described in this book, Virginity Code.

Ovarian Cyst

Female Ovarian Cysts and Cysts in between men's anus are in fact the human bodies way of attempting to get rid of bacteria and sexually transmitted bacteria from the human body.

If too many bacteria are taken in from too many sexual partners, or with one partner who has had a lot of sexual partners, one can get from that person a dose of bacteria that develops in their body cysts, and even cancer in the long run.

The penis and vagina not only retain STDs, but bacteria from every partner they have had sexual contact with, in the past. These little bacteria lay dormant and in the long-term create cysts and growths that need to be cut out if caught early enough.

However, generally, bacteria and the sexual karmic substances are a type of energy that do not disappear from the sexual reproductive region of the body and may mutate later and appear in other places of the human body after the growth, tumor or cysts are cut out surgically.

Sex and Auto-Immune Disorder

Your white blood cells and red blood cells may be out of wack leading you to an auto-immune disorder because you have had sex and are having casual sex and taking in other people's micro bacteria and possibly their dormant STDs as it weakens your immune system.

Hence, sometimes, the complex auto immune disorders that lead to many cartilage, kidney, skin and other issues are actually related to sexual misconduct.

This was common knowledge in ancient China in terms of a weakened immune system due to multiple casual sexual activity.

Of course, everyone is different, some may be able to take on a lot of sexual partners before their immune system is compromised. Each person's immune system is different.

Endometrial Cancer

The cells of the uterus can develop into cancer from STDs that are being exposed to multiple micro bacteria during casual sex, open relationships or simply, sleeping around.

Growth, tumors and the like can develop as well. Hence, it is always best to have only one partner for life who did not sleep around as it affects your future and family prospects.

STD Infects Pregnancy

Some children are born with one kidney or dysfunctional kidneys and there is no explanation other than it was a genetic defect.

But in fact, sometimes there are dormant STDs affecting not just the uterus and male sperm, rather micro bacteria from multiple sex partners living inside the intestines, skin and other parts of the mother that attack the baby's DNA building blocks from the male who has impregnated the mother.

This attack or hidden disease caused organs to not fully develop or for pregnancy issues to occur.

STD Passing on to Baby

Micro-Bacteria from previous sex partners like STDs can be passed on to the mother's child at childbirth or through the pregnancy.

Born with Mangled Head

The Uterus, in particular the endometrium can carry STDs or micro bacteria from multiple sex partners and spread throughout the uterus during a pregnancy.

This not only may get into the child's blood stream, but it may also cause defects in their look and shape when they are born.

The child may be born deformed, missing an organ, or with a certain growth on them because they were exposed to STDs and micro bacteria that were dormant in the mother and were activated during the pregnancy due to hormonal changes or a weakened immune system.

Worse, if the women cheated on the man, or the man cheated on the women during the pregnancy stage and introduced the virus and sexual bacteria to the womb and the baby.

Sharing Cups and Oral Sexual Disease

Ever consider where your mother's mouth has been? You sisters, father, grandmother, brother, friend, aunt, etc.?

Have you considered if they have performed oral sex or kissed someone who has an STD? Let's say you have an updated STD test on them that magically shows the dormant bacteria if any and you're sharing a drink together.

On that magical scenario, did they share a drink with someone else who had their mouth on who last night, last month, last year or a decade ago that caries their micro bacterial DNA and sexually transmitted diseases?

Even if it is not a sexually transmitted disease, ever consider you are allowing their micro DNA to enter you which carries their micro-bacterial health problems?

In that way, you are allowing their illnesses to enter you and replicate inside of you at the microlevel until it invades your immune system or becomes a part of your immune system as a foreign bacterial component digging at your own immune system and DNA.

Why do you think some kids naturally have an innate feeling of Qooties not just from the opposite sex, but from sharing drinks and saliva?

Sometimes, a kid with no degree has more intuitive common sense than your adults who may have a PhD and could be even a real Doctor. See, your PhD folks simply sat in buildings, read books, took tests and obtained their doctoral degrees.

Although it demonstrates a strong will to go through that boring and long process, the majority of today's PH.Ds are not like the original creative intellects of 100 years ago.

Hence, you must not and cannot depend on them for much of anything, as your garbage man may have more wisdom than they.

Best not to share cups with other people other than maybe 1 of your loved ones if you must, if both of you are healthy.

Sharing Food STD

As you are sharing food together you are breathing in and out particles and micro spit from your mouth into the same plate, food, fork or spoon.

Not only viruses can be spread, but sexually transmitted microparticles can be spread from the other person who has engaged in oral sex or even kissing with someone who was infected by a sexually transmitted disease or was involved with multiple partners who had the sharing of their bacteria transform *into an STD.*

Yes, as stated in the beginning of this book and revealed to everyone, a sexually transmitted disease can be created by 3 or more people who have sexual relations and share their bacteria.

And I do not necessarily mean a threesome which would in that case elevate the risk of a disease considerably.

Rather, when one person has sex with another and moves onto another person carrying the original persons micro bacterial elements inside their mouth, vagina, penis, or living within their skin, immune system, an STD can be created where one did not exist before.

Back Pain Sex Exhchange

The back pain a person has in their spine and other places is not simply due to a misaligned spine, a damaged nerve or from bad posture due to depression.

No, there is actually a bio-electrical field in the back of the human surrounding the protrusion.

In Eastern medicine and Qi Gong practice such as Falun Dafa, and Taoist internal alchemy, their literature states there is a black karma in the human body not just at the skin level, but the molecular and atomic layers causing the illnesses.

Meaning, the protrusion, tumor, growth is produced by a mass of black karma in the form of micro particles that flow and transport to the molecular level of your body affecting your organs, muscles, bones, blood, et.

In this case, you can take on a person's bad energy and back pain problems into your body not just by giving them a message, rather by hugging them long-term or having sexual relations with them.

You may not notice it if you have a very healthy back, and if the person you are messaging does not have a huge problem.

But, depending on the amount of exchange, you will feel it on your back, or in another place, in or on your body.

So, am I telling you not to message people and not to sleep around?

I am only sharing with you secrets that you can consider for your own well-being in this book and the well-being of others.

Modern medicine neither has the technology or intelligence to verify half of what I am disclosing in this book and in my videos and interviews that come from my experience, third eye and technology used.

Yet, in some way or another, most of what I say can be found in ancient cultures that had norms for making sure another person's sickness does not enter yours. It's just that I am explaining it much deeper and in a more concrete way from my experience, my third eye and technology used.

Karmic Emotional Trauma Transfer

Emotional trauma adds to a person's body, thoughts, mind, heart and spirit an invisible weight.

In particular, emotional trauma from failed relationships, people who have left you, abandoned you, betrayed or cheated on you, or simply gave you a lot of trouble.

This emotional trauma from a partner can come from a toxic person full of jealousy, pride, ego, selfishness, anger, and maybe even a drug addict and an alcoholic to boot who is on anti-depressants.

Whatever your emotional trauma may be, the more partners and the longer you are in that environment without attempting to remedy and grow positively from both parties, the more harm you will take.

This emotional trauma is in a form of an energy, a black karmic energy that carries inside a person's body, thoughts, emotions, mind, heart and sprit

This means, if you date or sleep with someone who has these emotional traumatic baggage's, their energy field which carries these toxins will affect you, go inside of you and hurt you to varying degrees.

You may not realize it, other than maybe feeling heavy or sad. Yet, it comes from that person and you sleeping around without an intention for a partner for life, or choosing one that is the right fit and will stick with you for life.

Are you saying when you have sex, or hug someone, their emotional trauma can transfer to you via energy and affect your negatively?

Yes, I am 100 percent saying that when you have sex with or hug someone, their emotional trauma can transfer to you via energy and affect you negatively and I am telling you it is a real concrete fact and a secret of the ages.

Many people suffer unknowingly when they form knew relationships and take on other people's energy out of marriage and casually date.

Of course, you could have the same toxins enter you in a monogamous relationship if the person has emotional trauma in their energy field because of sleeping around in the past, or because they were either born that way or went through a lot and may be did a lot of bad things in life.

Hence, choosing wisely is so important. Yet, almost all people have never worked on themselves in a very disciplined way to get rid of their vice and replace it with virtue.

This kind of discipline takes years, by the way. So, you always see a nice person with their best behavior until they get you in the relationship and after they get what they want, and only then do you see their negative side they hide from you either subconsciously, consciously or unconsciously.

ADHD Sexual Transfer

One's attention deficient disorder actually carries an electrical field in the brain, mind and body. If you have sex with this type of person, bit by bit some of that energy will transfer on to you.

On the other hand, if you do not have ADHD, or have a small case of it, the more sex you have with a person that doesn't love you and the more you sleep around, the more emotional trauma will be transferred onto you from each partner, adding to the weight, sadness and stress your mind already has in the long run.

You may feel okay and empty after the sex, but later it will show itself and increase your ADHD because you are not solving your emotional and mental issues that plagues you, rather you are adding others ADHD and emotional issues to yours.

You may say and believe you had ADHD upon birth, and that may be true, but the same chance of ADHD infection from other sexual partners exists for you.

Another may say, they don't feel it and they have had a lot of sexual partners.

Every person's mental and mind capacity is different, and it will eventually show later in life or affect you in another mental way, injuring your decision making or thought process.

Of course, there are those who are doing a lot of bad things, harmful to themselves and to others, and they don't feel a thing.

That is because their body and mind is in auto drive, kind of like a high, and they will only feel it years down the line when they overload the energy and health of their body.

This is why you see actors, musicians, and famous people looking great until one day they seem unrecognizable, with the loss of their beauty and health.

Hugs

Hugs by way of breath and sweat pores can transfer a cold, a virus or the flu. In ancient times it was common in civilized societies such as Persia and China where they had high levels of hygiene to keep space between people.

But did you know, energetically, hugs can transfer a bit of a person's mental, physical and spiritual illness as well as the person's state of mind?

It is said that people have a Qi Field, an Aura or an electrical field that is connected to their skin and pores as well as to other areas of their body.

Ever think how you can swipe your hand over your phone without touching it and make it do things?

The signals sent out from your brain, mind and body are in fact energy, and they carry your state of mind, sadness, mood, character and illnesses in various forms.

The electrical field in a human's body can infect and interact with your electrical field. And this holds true for the intrinsic energies that make up your soul, spirit or consciousness.

A man's intent, or a women's intent, whether unconsciously, subconsciously, or consciously can also be transferred on to you with a hug.

This means, the women or man can affect your thinking or decision making by their hug. The degree of the hugs' effect depends on the person's energy, the situation and timing.

In terms of the virginity code and hugs, hugs can sway a person's rational decision making to be swayed by emotions and the chemical reactions in the body to do something against the code or what one really wants.

Shaking Hands

A person's energy, electrical field, and normal bacteria can be transferred by a handshake. I will tell you, in my experience of traveling to 5 continents and over 37 countries, especially in America, at the very least, half the men do not wash their hands after using the bathroom.

The next time you are asked to shake a hand, know that you are touching something else, other bacteria and you may want to do a fist bump, or better yet, a martial arts bow like the ancient Chinese or a nod like the ancient Persians.

Cheating is a Crime

Within the Virginity Code, Cheating is like a crime. And if you think about it rationally, cheating is a crime.

Consider not just the amount of time, money, mind, soul and commitment people put into a relationship and for all that, including the developed interconnected relationships to be ruined.

Rather, think about how else it could be a crime where you are affected in a more concrete way that is more understood and still acceptable as a serious matter in today's lax moral society. And what is this crime?

If your partner cheats on you, and has sex with you passing on STDs, micro-bacteria, sweat poisoning from the foreign sex partner, all can affect your health.

Generally, the STD may be able to be proven, but certainly the black karma is beyond the comprehension and intelligence of today's judges, your Doctors and Ph.Ds., or at the very least, modern society within our scientific community does not have a recognized apparatus to very black karma.

Think about it further. If you cheat on someone, you are breaking their heart, giving them emotional trauma, and destroying all their time, youth, and vested commitment.

More so, the one who cheats lacks the intelligence and does not understand that inside the virginity code of the human body exists a program to harm oneself through depression, stress, sadness, mental trauma as well as the toxins that get released inside of the self from going against the universal cheat code and the virginity code.

You can say, the Universal Cheat Code is a punishment design within our own DNA programmed by the creator of humans.

Smokers STD

Did you know that smokers are reducing their immunity by smoking cigarettes, weed and the like while taking a hit on bongs and joints?

Let me tell you, they are also putting themselves at great risk to pass on or receive an STD or micro bacteria that can lead to a formation of an STD years down the line just by sharing the smoke, AKA drugs, together.

Vapes, Bongs, Joints, sharing of STDs.

At parties, private dates, with friends or people you are close to such as family and even at bars, restaurants and places of work the following may occur.

In your setting, wherever it may be, you may be sharing a vape that may or may not have marijuana in it. The micro bacteria on the vape or the STDs and saliva DNA of the person is also on that vape. And you are contaminating yourself with a possible dormant STD or live bacteria.

Joints will have a similar liability to passing on micro bacteria and STDs. So, the next time your friend offers you to take a hit from their joint, think twice and say no to the smokers STD.

You may be at home with a friend and taking bong hits together or at a party. A great deal of saliva is shared through that bong hit and you are taking in their micro bacteria which may infect you with foreign DNA affecting your immune system.

Worse, you may get an STD that shows up later in life just by sharing a bong, a joint or vape. Think about it, is that 1 minute high or the bonding you have with the other person that you think is or will be your friend as you are under the influence, worth getting an STD?

Is it worth it to not say no because you are afraid to not look cool, be accepted or hurt the other person's feelings, or in many regards, afraid not to get taken advantage of?

Yes, many people use weed and other smoke not just as a tool to bond, but to take advantage of you sexually or to convince you to have an open relationship or casual sex.

If you look at the restaurant, nightclub and bar industry scenes today, it is like that in many regards throughout the United States.

A drug culture in the bar industry filled with vaping, ecstasy, cocaine, adoral, and the like exist filled with STDs in open relationships, casual sex and border-line rape and manipulated sex or rape.

Chapter 3

RAPE: Bar Tender Manipulation

Bar tenders can be nice, witty, friendly, smiley and you feel like they are your pals that you can tell them anything, from your troubles, and at the same time have a great time drinking alcohol at their establishment.

You even think the association with the bar, or the bar tender will get you to sleep or have sex with the women or man you are interested in.

All these are possible and correct to varying degrees. But there is a sinister part to the bar tender life and some of their characters that move in the shadows unknown to many as it plagues not just the people, but the bar tender him or herself in daily life.

A bar tender can be an expert liar, and manipulator creating transactions for drugs, sex, prostitution, fights and the sale of some times illegal products beyond drugs as they influence not only the public, but the police and security that associate within their dealings.

A bar tender can be such as expert of a liar that he or she can look you straight in the face and lie as if they believe it and have 10 more lies to cover for the first lie to create a chain of events in order to accomplish something for him or herself.

What's worse, this trait and association of being an expert liar can and often does get passed on to other bartenders, and even their close families and friends through interaction and behavior exchange or contamination.

In terms of rape. Yes, bartenders manipulate, aid, and influence at the bars, and at house party's girls to like, trust or be influenced by another man that has the aim in having sex with them.

This interaction and team effort is not spoken of, rather most of the time it is a symbiotic relationship. Like on auto drive as if it is second nature to them.

They will either get the girl drunk, on drugs or with their sneaky words, flattery, and or putting the female in positions to be deceived, then get her raped.

Most of the rape is through intoxication, or the manipulation of the girl's mind and often times getting her hooked-on drugs such as Marijuana, Ecstasy, Cocaine, adoral and of the course the biggest one of all, alcohol.

Yes, bartenders are so well skilled, they will know what and how to mix what drink for a type of girl, personality and her body size in order to get her intoxicated enough to alter her brain chemistry so that she will consent without really consenting to sex.

Of course, this skill, throughout history has been used by evil men to rape a woman or get into their pants.

Without the alcohol and or drugs, they would usually have no chance as the female's brain would not be altered to go against her built in virginity code meant to protect her health, mind, body and spirit.

However, there are some bar tenders that will actively look for girls to get hooked on for their friends, associates, and or drug dealers, as is the case in night clubs.

RAPE: Friend Manipulation

Your friend or friends, can be a female or male, can, and sometimes do manipulate, influence or create the situations for you to be either raped or have sex with someone that you would not have originally consented to for any reason.

Sometimes this manipulation by a friend is subconscious or unconscious and they don't have really this plan to harm you, rather they are naive and a toxic person dependent on drugs, sex, alcohol and seek affirmation from their social network.

Other times, your friend or friends, out of jealousy, greed, or simply a toxic diabolical mindset create situations or set up with people in order to get someone to have sex with you without your true consent.

They, your friends, really aim to harm you and lower your character and state of mind.

Hence, they will say good things about a friend, a party or a group of people.

In addition, they will include influence through the group, music, the setting, shame, alcohol, drugs, smoke, peer pressure and physical gestures, touches, hugs, in order to loosen you up at a party or in a gathering.

RAPE: Party Manipulation

At a party, people will put up a front, with the aim to get sex, recognition, and have a good time as they are intoxicated with either drugs, alcohol, or certain smoke.

In fact, their sense of good time is an illusion if it involves drugs and alcohol since it is no longer them as their spirits are becoming numb.

Their real characters are not the ones talking and engaging, rather it's the intoxication or alcohol induced personality which is subpar, and garbage compared to those persons real true self, which is truly beautiful when you take away their vice and replace it with their innate virtues and positive characteristics.

However, that vice carries energy, and you will see that energy manifest in the party setting as the event, drugs and alcohol progresses throughout the night or event.

The energies of all the people at the party setting and the peer pressure can create obligated trust factors or situations where you are either slipped something or given too much to drink or become high enough for your brain chemistry to be altered.

Sometimes, marijuana and or cocaine is involved. Worse, you are foolish enough to cross fade with a drink and smoke of weed.

Through the interaction of the drugs, alcohol, peer pressure, and the energies present at the party, an awful situation is created where you are either raped, black out, or intoxicated and high enough to do things you would not do. Much like a mule, or an animal that salivates with food uncontrollably.

Later, you have emotional trauma and probably an STD, Micro Bacteria, or you cheat on a spouse and ruin your relationship.

The solution to prevent these types of rapes is to not associate with these types of people and don't attend parties where people will consume alcohol beyond 1-2 drinks and do not spend time with people who need alcohol and drugs at a party to have fun. If that can't be done, do not drink or do drugs at all.

Thus, the only way you could get hurt or raped is by either force, or if you are weak minded through influence and peer pressure at the parties or in association with these types of people, rather than merely under the influence of drugs or alcohol.

This is because some people do not require alcohol or drugs to be mentally influenced or manipulated into being raped.

They either are too trusting, insecure, unexperienced, naive or in a life situation where their depression has put them in a catatonic like state where they don't care and allow others to take advantage of them and use them per their need of social acceptance.

At times, the person allows themselves to be hurt or taken advantage of because they have so much black karma that they, in a crazy state do more bad things, or allow themselves to be used and suffer more pain in order to cover up the other pain they have or are going through.

This pain is kind of like an addiction, through self-destructive actions, going against the virginity code. They go through a cycle of sex, drugs, alcohol, video games, and other activities so they do not have a minute to feel or think about their pain.

The problem is, the more they do that, the more they add to their pain and fill their cup, their body with sickness, black karma, emotional trauma, as they harm their spirits.

Hence, best solution is abstinence from these sorts of parties and people who engage in casual sex and open relationships as well as drugs.

Because those people generally are addicted and their brain chemistry is altered to no longer value or understand what is right or wrong, as if they were a beast or an animal of low intelligence.

Losing all concepts of what it means to be noble and the joys of a sound mind, heart and spirit.

SEX & Losing Innocence

Have you noticed some children are very innocent not only in appearance, but in their minds and actions?

All human beings are actually supposed to be that way, rather than have characteristics innate in snakes, wolves and foxes that develop in people as defense mechanisms or the more numb they become through their unethical actions in life.

In terms of sex, the more sexual partners a person has, or masturbation and porn, the more that innocence in their mind and character disappears, and you will see that in their face if you have that experience and discernment.

The fact is, if it's not good for children, then why is it good for adults?

I don't mean sex here, rather the actions and behaviors that cause sexual, emotional and spiritual trauma for people who engage in casual sex, promiscuity or the unfortunate who get betrayed in a monogamous relationship.

Take for example, a girl that is 15-17 years old who has never had any sex with a bright face, skin with a rosy glow of health not requiring any make up whatso ever.

Soon after they sleep around, or include alcohol, drugs in their lives, their beautiful glow disappears, their pure mind and innocence is gone, and they develop emotional issues one after another.

This tells you, there is a virginity code in the DNA of the human body, and it is connected to the health in your skin, your immune system, your brain chemistry, emotional health and even your spirit.

All those positive virtues make up for your innocence, and once you lose it, it is so very hard to get it back unless you achieve sainthood.

Your innocence can even disappear in a monogamous relationship if your partner is filled with negative black energy, or his or her mind is filled with the micro bacteria and experiences of many partners and or pornography and masturbation.

`Porn and Virginity Code

Porn is the anthesis to the virginity code built into the human body as it destroys your health, mind, body and spirit.

Porn is the most destructive element today in society not only because it is for perverts, but if you ask anyone throughout history before casual sex was introduced in society by rock and roll, Hollywood, they will confirm it's unhealthy.

Porn teaches sex without love. And teaches sex that is nasty and degrading to females because it comes from a rapist mind.

Yes, those original creators of porn, had minds of rapists and looked upon women as animals they could exploit and use much like a slave.

Hence, when you view porn, you are emotionally, and energetically taking in their frame of mind, and altering your own thoughts, and the way your hormones and cells operate in your body. In turn ruining your own innocence, and stable state of mind.

Porn also is very addictive. If you watch it one time, the images you took in through your eyes replicate inside of your brain much like a virus.

Those porn images and their replications send signals to your privates and alter your brain chemistry to want more porn. That porn leads you to masturbation and or casual, open sex, in turn damaging your health, mind and spirit.

More so, porn will weaken your Qi, your energy, and make your mind be like a pervert through long term use. Have you noticed there is a great deal of child rape and child predators today than there were before the 1950s?

One of the reasons is porn, its addictions and the altered brain chemistry of the people who are addicted to the porn.

The other is, the creators of the porn not only had a rapist mind, but some of them were child predators or had those child fetishes, those sicknesses in their minds that got passed onto the porn industry.

Also, have you noticed that those who engage in the porn industry, die earlier of disease?

If not an STD or HIV, their other organs fail because porn and their casual sex with many partners destroyed their operating system that regulated the health of their organs.

Once a person's innocence is lost, and they become numb to sex, the next stage is the addiction to sex through multiple partners and the altering of their virginity code to something destructive and toxic.

The best way to prevent or recover from porn addiction is not ever watch porn, or lewd images, clips, movies that may lead your desire and mind to porn. Further, disassociate yourself from porn addicts, because their bad mojo will rub off on you.

Especially if they are big time porn masturbators. Their weakness and state of mind will influence and rub off on you. So, stay away from these people.

And if you are one of those people, and want to heal yourself, stop from all sexual activity and thought of sex for a few months or even a year of abstinence and fill yourself with virtuous music, exercise, hiking, meditation and do good deeds for others.

During your rehabilitation, stay away from the oppositive sex, platonic friendships, and of course, stop shaking people's hands, you masturbator you.

Disgusting. Especially when you know you didn't wash your hands, you nasty person you.

Real Friends VS Enemies

Real friends will never betray you. Real friends will be there for you when you need them.

More so, real friends will uplift you with good ethical and moral characteristics.

Real friends will tell you the truth, not use you, will not be jealous of you, and will be loyal to you as long as what you do is upright, honest and good.

Real friends will tell you what you are doing is destructive to you and others and attempt to help you get off your addictions.

Real friends will never offer you drugs, or marijuana, even if they are users themselves.

Because real friends would not want you to be addicted like them or to hurt you or bring you down to their level.

Of course, a real friend may tell you they have that addiction, and not bring it in your life and expect you not to judge them.

Enemies, or friends who act like enemies will be jealous of you. Enemies will try to get you to sleep around with risky behavior exposing you to sexually transmitted diseases, potential rape, or a multitude of emotional trauma.

Those who act like your enemies will offer you drugs and give you dose after dose of alcohol at a gathering, a party, in person or at a bar.

Enemies will not care about your health, or future, rather they will only care about the intoxication or high, destroying themselves in the long run or you.

Hence, choose your friends wisely. You may say, my friend is so nice, but yea, he offers me and exposed me to a lot of alcohol and drugs, and it was fun.

May be your friend was not aware that in a sense, they are being like an enemy rather than a friend who gives you positive lessons in life and uplifts you and allows both of you to grow together while you are having real fun.

SEX-PLATONIC FRIENDS

Throughout history, females and males were separated, and if together, they were supervised, or on double dates, or couples' night out.

If you saw a female and male together, it was because they were interested in each other. The past 2 generations, since the 1990s, and early 21st century, thoughts began to change.

Chris Rock spoke about platonic friendships, and as vulgar as it was, it is usually true because generally, a heterosexual, or bisexual female or male will have feelings at some point towards their friends at conscious, unconscious and subconscious levels.

Even if they claimed and claim that is not their interest, aim, intention, or desire to be anything more than friends by both parties involved and then believe in it wholeheartedly with a fighting emotion, unconscious, subconscious, conscious and situational elements always are at play or will be at play.

Take a woman for example. She may have 5 male friends she sees, 15-20 on Snap Chat she occasionally contacts. Or the number could just be a couple of male friends, a few more on Snap Chat and on Instagram.

If she claims they are just friends, or Ex boyfriends and she has no sexual desire for them, I guarantee you she does at the subconscious or unconscious levels, and or is lying to you in your face.

And if she is not lying, and not aware, the other party, meaning her male friends may create or are actively planning and trying to create situations for that emotion or activity to occur, or to get the female intoxicated.

Even if it takes a year, in that male's brain and hormones, that goal is there biologically, and consciously.

Sometimes the girl is insecure or had traumatic father issues or lack thereof, and she surrounds herself with boys or men. And sometimes, it's the men that pray on this type of girl and surround her. Either way, she is being preyed upon.

Of course, humans are humans. And a woman is capable of being just as bad as a man, but usually in a different way.

Men in history have overpowered their other gendered species by way of force, and when they have committed rape, it has been by force.

However, a girl or a woman can innately be as clever or more clever than an average men to use their looks, cuteness, sex and gender to get material positions, cheat men, and or lie and put other men in legal, and physical trouble.

You ask why they would do that?

Same reason a man would a hurt a woman. Humans can be bad, and have either mental illness, pent up anger, selfishness, greed, jealousy and the like.

Some women are misandrists, they generalize, hate and blame men for everything.

Some women have a partial dose of misandry inside them, and they enjoy playing the damsel in distress role while they one up and take advantage of men legally, financially or physically.

In history, men and even nations have fought over females, and not every time was it the fault of the women.

A woman can be an attention seeking personality, and create situations where men fight, or give her attention, even if she is married or in a relationship. And if she is single, it does not matter.

Whether single, married, or in a relationship, out of jealousy and the need for love and attention, a woman can set traps, cause discord and fights between other woman and even between men.

Some women are so sick in the head, that they crave causing others suffering and attempt to ruin relationships they deem happy.

Now, back to platonic relationships and the Virginity Code. If you want a faithful and bonding relationship beyond all others, both the male and female should not have platonic friends, and if friendly with the opposite sex, their significant others should be present.

This is because humans are not saints, and either the girl, or boy, or some outsider will unconsciously, subconsciously or consciously influence one of the two platonic friends to make sexual advances, or stimulate the other's emotions, hurting the other persons relationship in the short or long run.

If the platonic friendship includes marijuana, alcohol, and or anti-depressants, other mind-altering drugs as well as a bar, private or night club setting, the recipe for infidelity, betrayal or doing something you would never do, exists.

Also, having platonic relationships, exposes you to other men they will know, increasing your vulnerability. If you are a male, having more female friends, also increases the vulnerability of being influenced to either go against the Virginity Code, obtain an STD, or potentially cheat on your partner if you are in a relationship.

Finally, consider that the ancient people were not that backward. That may be, all these concepts of not having platonic friends if you are to be in a relationship or be married, have been tested throughout time.

Not having platonic friends, also includes not being casual in your speech and situational behavior with the opposite sex. This is a very important factor in fact. Ones speech, space, conduct and behavior with the opposite sex is very important.

Sex, Lies and Charm

Soon as you leave high school or home for a professional work environment, you will notice a different side of people. Professional, nice, may be charming with behaviors meant to keep business and operations proper with a chain of authority.

Did you ever think that most of the people in that profession today are fake mimicking the real characters of people from almost 75 years ago?

That is because for most of those professions, including doctors, attorneys, teachers, businessmen and the like, their characters 75 years ago were their own real home characters displayed at work. Their professionalism and way of talking was almost the same at home because it was an innate trait.

But today, people simply are not that way. Now, consider that element of fake acting at work, and consider just maybe a lot more acting is being done through sex, lies and charm.

A friend, woman, man, bar tender, server, salesperson, a family member, or just about anyone can lead their lives with a fake character dosed with charm and lies in order to get things.

What things? Attention, love, material positions, sex, drugs, acceptance, and everything else through manipulation.

Their lies and fake charm could be led by their conscious, subconscious or even their unconscious mind if they are not very stable and do not recognize where and how their thoughts, desires and emotions are formed, lacking self-control.

This charm can also be used to break through your virginity code, passing on disease, emotional trauma, financial hardship or put you in a situation you would not normally be in.

Generally, most people put on an act for the public with their clothes, smiles, voice, choice of words and behavior.

And when alone, or with people they have control over, they show their negative sides.

Thus, it is so vital to know and realize that your average kid in school, and adult in every profession can manipulate you with charm.

Manipulation through charm and lies can come from people in positions in society that are supposed to be just and of good character.

A judge, lawyer, police, politician, educator, server, military, doctor, and the like, all can have dual characters led by lies and charm to sustain their positions in society or in their attempt to get ahead in life by manipulating others as they seek favor.

There is another component to people who lead their lives with lies and charm. They could be very good to their family and friends and beasts to strangers, robbing them of everything. Or they could be great to strangers and beast to their own families and close friends.

These dual faced personalities drive their dual nature of lies, and truth, charm and character. Regardless of age, gender, race, they exist and to different degrees are traits in almost every human being on the planet.

These types of people are also in positions of entertainment and technology. The smart phones and IoTs you use, and their algorithms are designed to addict you, and hardwire your brain and biochemistry with the content you receive from dual personalities in the entertainment sector who lead their lives with lies and charm.

Hence, it is not only that you must watch out for the people you interact with in daily life, whether friend or foe, you must be aware of the content you take in from the entertainment and media industries and the people behind them.

This awareness of the lies and charm must be the case for the education system, the medical system, and everything you consume in life.

Because not many people in society are actively thinking and leading their lives with selflessness in an attempt to help others when they are in positions of power.

Cannabis Weed Smoke/Marijuana

Marihuana, Weed, Cannabis users will strongly fight and say Marijuana helps their chronic illnesses, and even Doctors and writers in media have been known to spout these theories without telling you the side effects, the real harm.

Let me tell you, it does not heal anything for them, rather it cuts off their senses like pain killers and creates a placebo relaxation state requiring the addict to have more and more bong hits, joints and vapes ruining their health, internal organs, brain, mind and clouding their spirit and consciousness with smoke. Giving away their true selves and free-will to the smoke.

Marijuana destroys your brain cells, blood capillaries, hardens the arteries and heart vessels, and damages your lung and heart in the long term. Increasing your risk of strokes, heart attacks, and what I call micro-amnesia.

This is where the weed user starts to forget bit by bit important things in their lives that sustain their health, relationships and life.

More so, marijuana, AKA cannabis, alters your brain chemistry and hardwires your brain weakening your will in the long-term making you unproductive and accepting of harmful people and behaviors in your life.

In particular, the altered brain chemistry on Marijuana contributes to one being more open in engaging in harmful sex acts, harmful unhygienic sexual practices, open relationship and casual relationships contributing to more emotional trauma and sexual transmitted diseases.

Of course, the relationships you have, the circle of friends that you have who smoke with you and may be drink with you, these relationships are not set on a healthy state of mind, and body, rather an interdependence of coping with each other's troubles by smoking your lives away.

Later, you will find that those people may not have been your friends if you were clear headed, or not good for you if you or they were clear headed from the start of your friendships.

Through meditation, herbal medicine, exercise, traditional arts, musical instruments, outdoor activities and Western medicine, and faith, one can at the very least cope and may even heal one's illnesses.

Rape by Weed/Drug Dealers.

Drug dealers and even those who sell Marijuana- Cannabis, can be and are for the most part, like rapists. If it's a man delivering drugs or selling drugs in States that allow growing and possession, but not selling, they are connected to rape, human trafficking and manipulated sex with the client.

If the girl is dependent on the weed, through social engineering, manipulation, and the guise of being friends, the drug dealer at some point gets sex.

This sex can turn into catching the client in illegal acts, indecent acts, where the client is put into a manipulative sexual dependency to the drug dealer and his or her so called friends, which are in essence, his or her accomplices. It becomes a form of slavery of the female's mind, body and spirit.

These drug dealers are some of the worst human beings on the planet. Because they ruin people, their clients, families and society at large, and actively engage in rape or manipulated rape through the selling of their drugs.

These drug dealers through time can turn the girl into a prostitute, or sex for favors, expected gifts, and exchanges which is a form of prostitution that the woman falls under.

The drug dealers, pretending to be a friend, can also video tape the client during sexual acts and alter the clients brain chemistry to think the sex and being casual through the drug dealers circle of friends is cool, or fun.

Because the girl is under the influence or dependency of drugs, alcohol and potentially anti-depressants, she fails to realize it or act and becomes numb and falls into almost a catatonic like codependent state with the drug dealers and his or her so called friends.

When this happens, the drug dealer can start the process of trafficking the girl even without the girl's knowledge.

Meaning, the girl will be manipulated through nonverbal threats of influence, drugs, co-dependency, and be trafficked to his or her friends as the drug dealer is making money without the knowledge of the girl.

However, at some point, through brain washing, drugs, being numb, and altered brain chemistry, the drug dealer may turn into the girl's pimp within his or her circle of friends, albeit a small operation.

These drug dealers ruin not only themselves, but the girls, families, and society.

I will tell you, if I was emperor, I'd have all these drug dealers that harm people, via mandate, skinned alive, and beheaded through compassion.

Weed whether legal Weed, or in illegal states, can also lead to alcoholism, Cocaine, Acid, Opium, Ecstasy, Heroin, adoral and other mind killing drugs.

No matter how much advocates of weed say it cannot or generally does not lead to other drugs, it does. All drugs and attachments to drugs lead to other negative and toxic attachments in one's life like branches in a tree.

Hence, it is very important to recognize drug dealers are not your friends and to watch out.

Main Spirit/Soul or Consciousness being Dulled

Casual promiscuous sex, in particular sex with multiple partners injures and dulls your spirit, soul and consciousness.

The karmic fields from your partners bio-electric fields infect and cloud the field around, on and inside your spirit.

Add drugs and alcohol to the mix, your spirit becomes more and more detached from your mind, brain and body.

When this happens, the casual sex, drugs and alcohol is still affecting your spirit. But, at this point, neither are you, your spirit, consciousness, brain or mind in control of your body. Then who is in control?

It is the person giving you the addictive materials, drugs and alcohol that is in control of you. You become a slave, and subject to rape, human trafficking, STDs, emotional trauma and a great deal of sin and black karma added to your bio-electrical field creating depression and even suicidal thoughts.

If you add marijuana, your risk of having more suicidal thoughts could actually increase, because the weed is clouding your judgment and separating your ethical mind from your spirit.

When this happens, suicidal thoughts and depression can increase. Especially if you are cross fading with alcohol and other drugs. Worse, if you are dumb enough to add cocaine, or opium to the mix when you already have suicidal thoughts or are very depressed.

SUICIDE, SEX, ALCOHOLISM, DRUGS.

After partaking in sex and activities you normally would not do if you were not influenced, manipulated, tricked or under the influence, you obtain more black karmic energy, in, around and on your body, and within your bio-electrical field. Creating more depression.

The more you live this type of life, and allow alcoholism, drugs and casual sex to take over your spirit, the more you allow the thoughts and energy that create the thoughts and feelings of wanting to commit suicide to grow within you, around you, and attached to your bio-electrical field that is connected to your thoughts, emotions and feelings.

To make a U-Turn and not let the thoughts and feelings of suicide take control of you, there are multiple steps to take.

Firstly, stop alcohol, drugs, casual sex and the associations with those people who partake in these activities and your so-called friends who have put you under their control or the under the control of the addictive substances.

Secondly, realize that those suicidal thoughts and feelings do not really come from you, rather from the black karmic energy in your bio-electrical field inside of you.

Thirdly, when you realize those thoughts and feelings are not you, begin to negate them with your own feelings, thoughts and words.

Tell yourself, it is not you that wants suicide and it is not a part of you. Expel those thoughts as time goes on. It may take you hours if you are very, very righteous with a strong will to expel that bioelectrical field and thoughts of suicide.

For most people, it may take days of great effort and mindful thoughts to repel it. With most, who take the normal approach of 30 minutes a day to a couple of hours, and who are of average will and mind, it will likely take them weeks to months to completely erase it from their mind, and field after they have given up alcohol and drugs.

For some, it will happen while they are giving up alcohol, drugs and casual sex. It really depends on how much of their bio-electrical field is comprised of thoughts, and actual energy that creates a field of suicidal thoughts, desires and feelings.

If they have had suicidal thoughts for years, and amassed a great deal of sinful, black karma or bio-electrical field from their emotional traumatic experiences, it will be more difficult and may take longer.

However, anything that is bad and is created can be eventually expelled and replaced with a positive element through work, effort, upgrading of one's moral and ethical character and relinquishing of one's vice.

Vice includes jealousy, selfishness, pride, ego, ignorance, anger, fear, lust, laziness and the very many addictive things one does, especially the addiction to TV, smart phones and video games that alter your brain chemistry to be hectically stressed and empty.

Finally, through this process, understand and consider if you commit suicide, anyone that loves you will be hurt greatly.

More importantly, if there is such a thing that your spirit does not die, if you commit suicide, you will not solve the issue that plagues you, rather add to it and your soul, consciousness and spirit would have even more pain.

Furthermore, if there is such a thing as enlightenment, awakening, salvation, or reaching a higher consciousness, you by succumbing to the thoughts of suicide would miss your chance at enlightenment.

And if there is such a thing as hell, or lower levels that are an awful existence for those who commit suicide, you should think even more about not succumbing to those thoughts of suicide that really are not from your own true mind and soul.

Know this, you are an incredibly special being, a human being with unlimited potential beyond what you are taught in school or on TV.

Do not allow that bio-electrical field that spews thoughts of suicide to sway you. It is not you, and in the grand scheme of things, once you expel it through some hardship, it is really nothing.

You have a chance to not only get rid of your depression, and suicidal thoughts, but you have a chance to take that struggle and tribulation, strengthen your will and go towards a path of enlightenment.

Anti-Depressants

Anti-Depressants can alter a person's brain chemistry to associate with corrupting people, be in a vulnerable setting or engage in sexual activities they normally would not engage in, or people they would not engage with sexually or emotionally.

Add alcohol, marijuana, Ecstasy, cocaine or any other drugs, and you will likely have an unstable self-destructive human being that will get taken advantage of by others and hurt others in return.

In particular, teenage girls or young women on anti-depressants are very vulnerable. Especially if Marijuana or alcohol is mixed in with anti-depressants, with an altered state of mind or altered brain chemistry

Usually, anti-depressants warn the patient on the label not to consume alcohol or engage in other drugs. Serious side effects can occur in addition to death.

These side effects include depression, mood swings, altered brain chemistry, impaired understanding, logic and reasoning.

Hence, Anti-Depressants are a vulnerability to the Virginity Code inside the human body and the many protective layers that exists for mind, body and spirit well-being when mixed with alcohol and drugs, and sometimes even by themselves.

Alcohol

In ancient Persian faiths of Zoroastrianism and Mithraism that spawned Catholicism in Rome mixed with Judaism, it was said the spirit is injured by the consumption of alcohol and that it is the "Devils Brew".

In Eastern Medicine, especially in the Taoist, and Falun Dafa Qi Gong Literature, it is said alcohol disrupts and blocks the flow of energy, the Qi that flows in between the organs, skin, bones, and even in your hair, with long-term consumption of alcohol leading not just to health issues, but a weakening of the mind, body, sprit and one's morals as guided by virtue.

The biggest risk to the human body's virginity code, is in fact alcohol. Men have used it to disarm a woman and get her to have sex with them throughout history.

In fact, sometimes, the use of alcohol by a man to get a women drunk with the aim of having sex with them can be construed as pre-meditated rape.

Because alcohol causes a chemical imbalance in the human brain, destroying the human's ability to have reason and logic as their guide. Instead, the carnal desires are activated much as a beast or animal would salivate or be activated in heat.

However, for a woman, a girl, alcohol can and has been used against them as a weapon to alter their perception, emotions, mood, mind, thoughts, brain chemistry and dumb down their spirit in order to penetrate them.

Thus, if a person is to have sex for the first time with someone, it is best neither party has had consumed any alcohol. This way the question of consent, right, and if the parties really have anything lasting in common, including values, shall have a chance to exist.

Alcohol is also extremely addicting and our society since the failures of prohibition has created functional alcoholics, (Functional Alcoholic is someone who is an alcoholic but goes to work, and most people may not see or realize that this person is an alcoholic, yet they may be enabling and influencing others, including their family members to be alcoholics) alcoholics and the occasional influenced and drunks as a cultural foundation to socialization for young and old, especially in America.

Persia, Rome and Greece were all destroyed with the aid of alcoholism, lust, jealousy, casual sex and pride as the root of their vices and decay, prior to their plagues, and wars that led to their invasions, enslavement and deaths.

I question the reader and audience, why do human beings need alcohol to socialize?

Are people's characters lacking in virtue, quality, spunk, fun and the intelligence that they need to consume a beverage like alcohol that is poisonous to the human liver, heart, brain, nervous system, and truly the human spirit?

Are people that dull, and their characters need to be lifted by Alcohol at social gatherings, parties, taverns? What about Juice, Tea, Water, Smoothies?

From a higher level of consciousness and intelligence beyond the human race, if you look at human beings sitting around consuming poison to alter their feelings and perceptions, it is as if we are looking at unintelligent baboons fighting and jumping around.

Of course, one will not agree with this assessment if they fall into a lower category of intelligence, regardless if they are a drinker or not.

Some are big drinkers, and they know it's a dumb ass thing to do, but they are addicted and too weak to alter their paths of alcoholism and too entrenched with a field of sadness and as the Eastern meditators say, Black Karma and depression. It is a very difficult thing to overcome, yet it can be done.

You can smile, laugh, have fun without alcohol and obtain real genuine friendships with genuine people who are stable and not controlled by the mind dumbing substances we call bear, liquor and alcohol.

There was a huge reason for the Temperance Movement that took the globe by storm, leading to prohibition, meant to free people and their families from the illnesses of alcoholism.

Yet, some bankers who controlled half the world at the time purposely aided in sinking the economies of the Western world and supported the alcohol industries and gangsters behind them in order to gain control over multiple interconnected industries in people's lives.

Later, when alcohol became legal, their strength grew tremendously and towns, cities and regions were filled with bars and nightclubs replacing much of the traditional family life that excluded alcohol and its control over people.

In order to stop alcoholism, one should also realize how historically it has aided in sinking economies, families, societies and civilizations such as Persia, Rome and Greece.

The trick is to stop consuming any and all alcohol because just one sip sparks the addictive nerves and a vodka, liquor lover, or that urge for that bottle of wine, or 8-10 glasses of beer will resurge.

But how can a person stop alcohol all at once?

If you can't, you lower the amount day by day, until you reach zero and stay at zero.

However, there is a trick to stopping alcoholism.

COMPLETELY DISASSOCIATE FROM ALL PEOPLE AROUND YOU WHO DRINK AND ENABLE YOU TO DRINK, NO MATTER IF THEY ARE YOUR FAMILY OR FRIENDS. PRIOR TO DOING THIS, MAKE SURE YOU HAVE SAFETY AND SECURITY IN EVERY WAY POSSIBLE.

UNTIL YOU ARE THE MASTER OF YOUR OWN LIFE, STAY AWAY FROM THE ALCHOLOICS OF ALL FORMS AND SOCIAL DRINKERS OF ALL FORMS.

Cross Fading

Cross Fading is when a person attempts to have what you could say is a double high from Marijuana and alcohol at the same time. At times, consuming a great deal of liquor and smoking a great deal of marijuana.

Even a little bit of a mix can alter the brain chemistry of the person and put them in vulnerable sexual situations, trafficking, and even suicide. Mix in anti-depressants with alcohol and weed, that combination is even worse.

I would say, we can term it, Dumb Ass Fading instead of cross fading when an individual mixes multiple drugs for a high.

It is utterly dangerous, damaging to the brain and one's organs and overly destructive to the virginity codes mind-body health defense mechanism.

Chapter 4

Casual Sex

The concept of casual sex is anthesis to the virginity code, and creates the opportunity to develop multiple physical, emotional, mental and spiritual illnesses. Often, casual sex is imbedded into the term "Open Relationship"

Open Relationship

Open relationships were practiced by evil religions, religions where the man had more than 1 wife, or by conquering armies who created communities after their rape and pillaging stages normalized within the invaded culture.

The same mindset of infidelity, rape, pillaging, greed, and fear of losing a committed relationship some how has been dumbed down to a friendly term called "Open Relationship" by a group of toxic people who have repackaged polygamy into a clever system.

However, too often, those who have accepted open relationships or have been subject to one with manipulation of their emotions or simple fear, have not realized where it stems from and how toxic an open relationship is physically, emotionally, mentally and spiritually.

It's a term, a system designed for cheaters, and those who fear or are incapable of obtaining a loving relationship. More so, in an open relationship, the chance of catching an STD or creating one with the exchange of bacterial particles between the sexual human hosts increases dramatically.

Purification of Sexual Karma/STD/Energy

How do you erase, delete, get rid of all the messages, energetic karma, emotional trauma and STDs that exist inside of the human flesh body as if you were a new-born baby?

You cannot unless your physical body reaches a divine level at or above the level of a real saint with divine powers, a Buddha, an Angel or a God with purification. *What do I mean by this?*

Well, this is so deep and almost impossible unless you no longer desire sex or carry any human vices in your mind and have transformed your body physically through the paths of ancient catholic saints, or a Taoist, Buddhist Qi Gong advanced disciple in Falun Dafa, or if lucky enough, a living

God shows up and purifies you at the molecular level, layer by layer getting rid of your sickness.

If you are able to achieve enlightenment, or awakening, then only at that point can you reset your body to where it was when you were a newborn and beyond.

Well, since it is almost impossible, what else can you do?

Other than treating STDs the normal medical way, you can abstain from sexual conduct and any sexual thoughts for 6 months, to over 1-2 years, and reduce your vices like jealousy, lust, pride, arrogance, selfishness, ego and fear. In this way, your mind and body will begin to transform a bit more and heal to varying degrees.

Sexual Body Counts

The number of people a person has slept with is materially existing inside their body, energy, brain, mind and attached to their spirit.

To varying degrees, you take on health issues, characteristics, emotions, thoughts, micro bacteria, STDs, and the Black Karma of each person you have ever slept with in this lifetime.

And if you believe in reincarnation, or being reborn, than if you have had a past, that also exists in your body as well.

And if true, this also explains why some people are born innately with negative sexual characteristics, and a great deal of sexual lust, deception, or even sickness.

What is even worse is that each person you slept with, their body counts that contain their negative elements of micro-bacteria, health issues, bio-electrical field, and black karma also get added up to a lesser degree, and get transformed to you as well.

Your Partners Body Count Adds to Yours

For example, if you slept with 10 people, you get a huge dose of black karma from each person to varying degrees, and to lessor degrees smaller doses of each person those 10 had slept with and beyond.

Hence, in a way, if those people slept with 30, in some energetic senses your number goes up to 10 plus 30, equaling 40 in energetic black karma you receive.

Now, if it is an STD, it gets transferred straight through each person with some showing signs of contamination and some not because it is dormant in their bodies.

As explained in this book virginity code, toxic and poisonous elements from emotions, thoughts, STDs, micro-bacteria, skin health exchange, sweat pore poisoning, intestinal health exchange, saliva, heart, kidney, lung and other organs health issues all get transferred bio-electrically as well as through DNA and bacteria.

Spiritually giving you an unclean soul riddled with mental trauma with an unclear consciousness.

Body Count Relationship Matching

A person's body count as described in this book Virginity Code consists of a complicated number of toxic elements that makes the possibility of a successful loving relationship as well as their future health and happiness more difficult and in some cases almost impossible.

These toxic elements within the virginity code include micro-bacteria from all their partners, emotional trauma, electromagnetic frequency exchange, intestinal exchange, skin health exchange, potential STDs, sweat pore poisoning, heart and other organ health exchange, Black Karmic energy field and degrees of broken hearts to a sense of sorrow from being dumbed down through multiple partners and relationships.

The number of sexual partners a person has affects the amount of black karma, mental, emotional, physical and spiritual disease they carry within them throughout their lives and the prospects of a happy life.

The less body count with people who were not only healthy but carried pure and positive energy with lower black karmic energy, the better for you.

However, body counts or number of sexual partners a person has is not the ultimate guide or an ultimate assessment criterion to determine how healthy they are or how much of a match they are with you and you with them.

It is rather an important tool and data that must be assessed with other criteria's within not only the body count, but compatibilities of interests, biochemistry, love, body, mind and spirit for the perfect match.

For example, not only the number of people you have had sex with, but the quantity, amount of time, the connection, and how much each of your partners carried black karmic energy within their bodies and how many partners they had, and the gamete of sexual micro-bacteria and toxic elements exchanged with you, play a huge role.

An additional factor exists not determined by sexual partners. That is, a virgin could be born with a great deal of black karmic energy, an unhealthy body, just like people are born with cancer and so on.

And that could be because that person carries a great of black karmic energy from a past life, being reborn, or within their genetics and ancestry blood lines.

A person carrying a great deal of black karma as a virgin could be like picking a mate that has had 10, 20, or even 50 partners full of emotional trauma, instability, micro-bacteria, and black energetic karma.

Hence, in life, the search for the perfect mate that matches you and will stick with you, and meld well with you is such a difficult thing to accomplish.

And even if you are successful, there are bad things that happen in life or the negative destinies that exist in your life, your family, social community and society at large.

That being said, it doesn't mean that one cannot do better and find a better mate by understanding the virginity code and upgrading their ethics and morals to reduce the chances of obtaining illnesses, depression, and a huge load of black karmic energy through casual sex that will hurt your body, mind and spirit.

This is where body count and understanding plays a very important role in your decision making and match making.

This is just a guide on sex body count numbers, not counting time, quality and the amount of black Karma, and bacterial particles in each human host's body.

0-1

Zero to one sexual partner is best suited for 0-1, may be 2-3, unless the partner with 3-6 past partners has great qualities of character, and good energy, and did not engage in much activity with most.

1-3

One to three would be similar to 0-1 partners, yet more leeway and less strict with the partner of more body counts to outweigh his body counts vice by providing great energy and great character qualities.

4-10

Four to five, would be similar to 1-3 guidelines, however, the other partner may be able to have 10 or so partners and provide a great character.

5-10

Five to ten partners is getting into a higher unstable category. Best these people have partners with similar numbers, maybe up to 15 or so.

10-20

Ten to twenty is a significant number, with that person carrying more than the usual Karmic field, and requiring someone similar in numbers, and may be allowed to reach 30 or so.

20-30

A person with 20-30 partners is in a different category, and is surely to be filled with more difficulties, getting close to a point that their human nature will alter.

30-100

Persons with 30-100 are about to enter a point of no return, filled with a great deal of black bio-electrical karma, emotional trauma, micro bacteria and dormant STDs if no STDs are present currently on tests. They are likely almost numb to true human love.

100, 500, 1000 and more.

I have interviewed people that have been with up to 5,000 people, and many who have had 100-200 partners. Non were prostitutes, yet all of them had huge black karmic fields as well as great emotional trauma and many addictions to alcohol, drugs, porn and the like.

With exception to just a few who still had a supply of positive bioelectrical energy field that had not run out as they were being depleted by the negative karmic exchange of one partner after another.

Those people were born with a great supply of positive energy field, and it took longer and more partners to dry them out of their virtue, good luck and positive energy. Very difficult to match with these types of people who have such huge numbers of sexual partners unless you yourself are in that category of numbers.

Multiple Partner Sex Capacity.

You may ask, why are there some people who can have sex with 20, 50, 100, 200, or more people and seem not have any diseases, or much affected emotionally, physically, or mentally and may seem happy?

It is because each person is born with a certain amount of positive QI, life force, or bioelectrical field, and strength in immunity as well as stamina and organ health.

For these people, they have to deplete their Qi, their bioelectrical field, as well as their stamina and organ health before their trauma, sickness and other issues catch up with them.

However, there are some special cases, that when the person's positive energies and positive immunities dry up, their negative energies, and sickness as well as parasitical sexual bacteria take over their body and mind.

When the parasitical sexual bacteria as well as their black karma take over their body and mind, they obtain further drive, and stamina to conquer and have more casual sex with other partners as they spread their disease, parasitical bacteria and black karmic energy until finally it catches up with them, and they get sick, change their ways or die.

Bio-Electrical Field Exchange

When a man and women get together to have sex or some type of sexual interaction, they are not only risking contaminating each other with STDs, micro-bacteria, bio-electrical diseases, rather they are exchanging each other's bio-electrical fields.

Whatever qualities make up each person's bio-electrical field gets mixed with the partners and an exchange process exists.

If a partner has many great qualities inside their energy field, their partner can be exposed to that positive energy and get some of their good bio-electrical components at the same time getting their negative and bad bio-electrical components.

However, every human being is different and carries different amounts of toxic vs positive qualities within their bioelectrical field.

You will generally not know what your partner carries. Thus, it is best to assess not just their character, but to pick and stay with one so you are not exposed to extra and additional bio-electrical fields that will infect, contaminate and negatively affect your health and bio-electrical field.

This is because your body, its bioelectrical field and energy patterns are unique to you. The more bio-electrical exposure you add to yourself with various partners, the more foreign energy fields will disrupt your energy field, mind, body, and spirit.

Emotional Energy

Emotions are an actual energy as well that form thoughts and, in another sense, can be formed by thoughts as well.

Usually emotions are fading, unstable, and sometimes toxic. Emotions can also cause anger, instability, addictions and lead you to make bad decisions.

You sexual partners emotions can not only affect you when you are with them, or associated with them, rather having sexual relations with them creates a symbiotic relationship allowing their emotions to be transferred into you and yours to them. And I do not necessarily mean love, bliss and sex here. No, I mean their traumatic emotions, toxic emotions and instabilities.

Thought Exchange

The thoughts that exist in your partner's brain, mind, body and energy field can be transferred on to you and you may telepathically feel it at the subconscious level unless your ESP is very strong. After their thoughts go into you, your values can exchange or be corrupted.

Value Exchange

If your partner has great values, character and special qualities to them, through sex, some of their energy will not only affect you, but it will transform you. You will obtain their values, whether positive or negative.

If your partner is corrupting and immoral, their values also energetically get transferred into you bit by bit through sex.

So, be very careful here. Your bioelectrical energy field is precious and makes up how you feel, your thoughts, happiness, and even your destiny to varying degrees.

Evil-VS Good Exchange

Your body has a bio-electrical energy field, and that field can be denoted by positivity, vs negativity, good vs evil.

The amount of energy that is good and bad is also contained within your energy field, and it is expressed in your character, mind and spirit as well.

If you have sex with someone who has more evil or bad energy inside them and let's say you are 50/50 on your end with 50 percent bad and 50 percent good, you are tipping the scale and becoming a worse person.

And when you become worse, you will do more bad things, harming yourself, creating more depression and sadness within yourself, adding to the black karmic bio-electrical field you have.

If you take in too much of an evil energy field, you may not only do evil things in terms of sexual conduct. You may do evil things in your daily life in how you treat others or how you do business, taking advantage of others and increasing your own pain and hurt, as well as others.

If you take in a great deal of evil energy, you may become an evil person in every regard. The balance may even tip from suicide, to murder, robbery, rape and the like.

Hence, it is very important to follow the virginity code, not sleep around and certainly find the best match for yourself.

Now, if you think you can find a very pure and innocent person, to fill yourself with more good energy, and alter yourself, think again.

The codes and energy field in their body will reject you because you cannot do so many bad things and expect to get away with your bad conduct and simply replace your bad energy with someone else's good energy. The universal code will not allow that.

However, if it's natural, and you both provide positive exchanges of energy, your energy can provide some good things for her and her for you as long as there isn't a huge gap in between the amount of sexual activity and partners you had.

If she has had 1-2, and you have had 20-40, it certainly will not work and your energies will never match no matter how you feel about each other, unless the person who has had 1-2 partners was born with a great deal of negative bio-electrical field matching your bio-electrical field comprised of 20-40 partners.

Depression Exchange

If a person is depressed, that depression is coded and exists as a black karmic energy inside their bio-electric energy field.

The more promiscuous sex they have, the more they add to their depression for two main reasons that connect to sub reasons.

Reason one, is that they are breaking the virginity code in the body meant for the union of a life partner, childbirth, love, and spiritual perfection as designed and coded in the human body.

When you go against this innate program, like a virus, depression is created inside of you and multiplies in addition to other types of depression that exist, or you may have already had since birth innately programmed into you to appear sometime in your teenage years or later.

Of course, your environment, social, financial and health status plays a role in that depression, and that too can be a program at a higher level beyond most people's comprehension as to why, how, when and for what reasons.

If you have sex with a very depressed person, their depression is actually energetic and a form of a bioelectric substance, or black karmic field. Through hugs, kisses, and sexual conduct, you will obtain some of their depression.

Karma/Sin Exchange

Through sexual contact or mating, you will exchange your negative black karma or the sin that exists in your body with your partner and vice versa, affecting both your health, mind, body and spirit.

From a spiritual or religious perspective, people are either born with karma and sin, they accrue it from birth, or from both a past and birth.

In the Eastern and old Persian and Greek faiths, you were born with sin and karma because your spirit did not begin its journey with this life, rather it moved on one life after another in the different layers of heavens, hells, and mortal planes of our universe.

In the Jewish, Semitic traditions of Islam, Christianity and Judaism, you accrue sin even though you may have been forgiven or your sins were born by the Savior, Jesus, yet the teachings are not clear that you had a spirit in the past other passages about being "Fallen". However, if you think about it deeply, and awaken to it, it really means the same.

However, more intelligent and advanced spiritual cultivators in Catholicism, know that if there is purgatory, it is because they have come to the self-realization that in order to have faith in Jesus, other angels or God, they must achieve awakening and purification through discarding not only sin, but attachment.

When they get to that level, they actually reach the realm of thought of Taoist, Buddhist, Falun Dafa, Ancient Zoroastrianism, Celtic, Nordic and Greek traditions which clearly explained that you must put down your vice and achieve enlightenment to enter realms beyond this universe that are not subject to suffering, pain and death.

That simply proclaiming your belief in a savior and being a "Sinner" who lies, cheats, has fear, lust, pride, ego, jealousy will not earn you heaven no matter how many times you attend a church.

Because why would heaven allow someone of this caliber to be there?

Why would your life start here in this mortal world full of suffering, pain and a journey instead of being born in heaven?

Then one thinks further, and kind of figures out, ah, what does it really mean through faith. Well, I did about the age of 12 years of age. I figured this out after a lot of thinking you could say.

Claims of Stomach Aches

Lots of people claim they have stomach aches that they do not understand how and why it developed.

Stomach pains can be from fear, worry, stress, or emotional trauma from being harmed or harming others.

I will share with you, there is an intestinal exchange that gives you this stomach pain through sex, particularly having sex with multiple partners, or in an open relationship. Let me explain in the next section.

Intestinal Sex Exchange-

When you have sex with another human being, you are in fact exchanging your intestines. Yet, exchanging your intestines at a physical, electrical, karmic, emotional and energetic level reaching the spiritual realms.

Most of this exchange of your intestines through sex is very sickening if I delved too deep. So let me just reveal to you the important aspect of sex and your intestines so you will be forewarned for your health the next time you choose a partner or decide to have casual sex or be in an open relationship.

At the micro-bacterial level, the intestines reach your skin, pores, anus, and private parts such as your vagina and penis.

The micro-bacterial particles in your intestines exchange with your sexual partner through your skin, sweat, and fluid exchange. Even through a kiss.

Yes, with a kiss, the gas substances that exist in your stomach flow through your breath, and the micro-bacteria up your esophagus into your mouth, and infect your partner you kiss, give oral sex to and have sex with, infecting and mixing both human beings DNA.

Now, what is the danger of exchanging your micro-bacterial particles with multiple sex partners or just one?

If it is only one person, and the person has very bad intestinal issues, with a chronic disease, depending on your immune system and the energy in your body, their unhealthy state may and will affect your intestines to varying degrees.

If you have sex with multiple partners, you are exchanging the karmic energy, and micro-bacterial intestinal particles of multiple people and the people they had sex with and putting it into your body, creating the physical situation where sickness may be created in the long term inside of your body.

Thus, chronic IBS, stomach aches, trouble eating, digestive issues, and even stomach cancer can develop late in one's life by mixing your body with the wrong people or too many sexual partners.

Now, this situation of intestinal sexual infection as said will affect each person differently because every person is born with different levels of immunity and has different strengths and as the Eastern practices say, Qi Potency.

If the person has strong positive Qi or energy, that strong and clean Qi will have to run out first until the sicknesses they took into their body transforms past their immunity barriers and affects their health appearing as a concrete sickness modern medicine and its technology can detect.

Skin Health Exchange

The smoothness of your skin has to do with the health of your liver, heart and kidneys and if they are not being obstructed by certain lifestyles and unhealthy activities.

If you have healthy skin, and your partner does not, it is because one or more of their organs are not functioning at optimum.

Also, their quality of life, food, mental wellbeing may not be harmonized with a possible sickness existing in their skin organism preventing cellular cohesion.

Through sex with a partner who has unhealthy skin, the micro-bacterial particles that make their skin unhealthy through time can affect your skin.

More importantly, their organs that are dysfunctional, through time can affect your organs.

Of course, the strength of your immunity, Qi of your organs, DNA, age, lifestyle, food intake, has a lot to do with how, when and how much you are affected.

The most important takeaway for keeping your good skin would be to not have sex with multiple partners because you are exchanging and contaminating your skins unique organisms by who you sleep with and who you are touching, kissing and having sex with throughout your lives.

In fact, the human skin is designed to be smooth, glow, and healthy without needing make up. It is lack of knowledge, and going against the virginity code as described in this book that affects the health of one's skin.

Of course, the health of one's mind, functioning of one's organs, and really, the prowess of one's spirit, has a real-world effect on the look and health of your skin.

Sweat Pore Poisoning

The human sweat pore is designed to breathe in the air in a very sophisticated way different from the lungs as well as to expel poisonous human and non-human toxins through both visible and invisible sweat.

Through touching, even if you are playing basketball, or touching another person, their sweat or yours can pass on toxins to them.

However, through sex and making out, when your skins are touching, the micro-bacteria particles and poisonous elements enter both partners, causing not just health issues, but affect the person's mind.

Because sweat can carry an exorbitant number of micro bacteria that the human body has dissolved and prepared to expel. And this sweat, instead of being sweated out through exercise, or normal walking, sleeping and sitting activities, is shared and put into your sexual partner.

Hence, it is best to follow the virginity code not simply because of STD's and trauma risks from sleeping around, but from avoiding the micro-poisons that emit from a person's skin through sex. Best to pick one suitable partner for life, which is very hard to do.

Micro-Organisms Living on Skin

Every person sheds skin on a daily basis with microorganisms living on their skin that feed off the person and are generally not very healthy for the host human who has them and more so for a foreign human body to be exposed to these micro-skin organisms.

If you had a magnifier, you would see something like an insect crawling all over people's skin. These microorganisms when mixed with other people's microorganisms can create other microorganisms if exposed to multiple sexual partners different microorganisms.

Moreover, these microorganisms can produce an STD on the skin. They can create it from skin to skin contact if multiple people are involved, as well as the poisonous substances on a person's sweat.

Of course, a baboon or a low-level animal would not believe or even think of the things I am mentioning in this book and would not believe it.

But an open-minded human would believe it and would be very appreciative of the knowledge in this book, Virginity Code.

However, there are some animals, who instinctively know this, and do not sleep around. They are even more wise than some people with regard to monogamy.

In fact, some Swans have mates for life for varying reasons. And other animals, such as lions and wolves, they can smell and detect if other males have mated with the females they are attempting to acquire.

This is not simply out of power, or jealousy, rather it is a health code programmed in some animals to varying degrees.

In the human body, this health code, which I call the Virginity Code is extremely sophisticated and numerous if you sleep around with multiple people.

The program and code designed in the human body is not like animals, rather it is something solemn, and meant for spiritual perfection and the achievement of a higher consciousness.

Chapter 5

Virginity in Antiquity and Folklore

Persian Virginity

The dignity, nobleness, character, statues and ability to have healthy kids was a key component in Persia's cultural heritage. If a women or man broke promiscuity laws, they would be banished or executed.

It was said that a pure person, or a pure women would not need make up and their skin would be glowing like a newborn baby of health and clarity.

This was the belief in ancient Persian heritage, and virginity and abstinence from sexual activity was part of this ability to "Glow" according to oral traditions passed down in the many tribes of Iran since one Persian Dynasty after another.

The glow in the face and teachings of the ills of promiscuity started at the state level with Cyrus the Great in the age of the Achaemenid around 550BCE, to the Parthians and

Sassanians who passed on Mithraism, culture and law to the Romans that took shape in Catholicism. If a person broke promiscuity laws, they would be executed and bound for hell.

Catholic Virginity

In the Catholic faith, where much was derived from Persian Zoroastrainsim and Mithraism through Rome, virginity was not only valued for a person's character, purity and ability to be loyal, rather it depended on one's salvation.

It was believed if you broke the sanctity of marriage, you would be bound for hell by breaking promiscuity laws.

This was also true not only in all Abrahamic faiths derived from the Jewish semitic tribes such as Judaism, Islam and eventually Christianity, rather in the Aryan Nordic faiths of Zoroastrianism, and the many pagan faiths of the Nordic Viking and Celtic tribes.

Viking/Celtic Virginity

In the Viking faith, a women's womb was seen as a holy place. If a men or women broke their promiscuity laws, they would be put to death and not have the ability to enter heaven.

The Celtics valued it so much that they used it as a battling cry against the invading roman armies until they were subdued. This was also the case in their rebellion against the English invaders.

China Virginity

In China, Virginity was prized for the purity in one's body, as well as the pure Qi in a body of a person who did not sleep around, as well as a set standard to be able to enter heaven.

Promiscuity laws that were broken were met with execution. This was the case since the Qin Dynasty as well as the Tang Dynasty.

Yet, today in Communist China, the CCP (Chinese Communist Party) promotes casual sex and at the same time forced abortion, sterilization and contraception to keep the population low and control the people with the Marxist doctrine of violence and authority.

Taoism Virginity

In Taoist internal alchemy, your vital essence is needed to transform your Qi and physical body. The more pure and innocent your vital essence was, the easier it was to transform you Qi for spiritual perfection.

The old book Tao Te Jing from 2500 years ago has passages hinting to this, and this explains Zhuan Falun's take on using vital essence to transform your spiritual body for enlightenment with the requirement of a pure mind and body.

Zhuan Falun is the text by Falun Dafa which incorporates Taoism and Buddhism and a form of Catholicism for saints. That would be the shortest way to describe it here in terms of its relation to vital essence and antiquity. The book is vast on the topic of body transformation and the value of purity.

Japan Virginity

In Japan, and every nation I have mentioned thus far, one's purity was one of most importance for divine purposes within Buddhism. A female would rather kill herself bound for hell, than be allowed to be raped. It was that serious.

Although there are many more cultures, nations and faiths, here I described in short, the importance of the virginity code in antiquity with questions.

Was it passed down by Angels, Buddhas, Gods or the Creator?

Or is it that simple and illogical that the ancients would find casual sex a sin and ironically their notions made sense in terms of Sexual Transmitted Diseases and emotional trauma from multiple partners?

Or is a the virginity code a program design by the creator of humans on this planet and mortal dimension where sex exists?

Is there such a thing as having a pure body and mind in order to achieve a higher enlightenment, salvation, awakening or consciousness and does it relate to the virginity code?

I say, without a doubt, the Virginity Code was designed by the creator of humans, and this universe and there is a relationship with how pure one's body, mind and spirit is in relation to one's ability to achieve salvation, awakening, a higher consciousness or enlightenment.

Masturbation Anti-Sex Code

For many reasons, the ancients stated that masturbation is not only unhealthy, but weakens a person and reduces one's lifespan making them look and feel unhealthy.

In the spiritual community such as the Sufis, hidden works of Rumi, Falun Dafa Qi Gong, the path of Saints in the faith of Catholicism, it was said that the person would be empty of spirit and mind, or of low frequency and character if they engaged in masturbation or too much sex.

Not being able to achieve a divine state beyond the human state of sex, food and socialization which the majority partake in their entire lives or attempt to have a better life with nice things, good food, sex, money and good social friendships.

The ancient Persians had a saying for their champions "His fluids have dried up through masturbation and too much sex". This is a rough translation of what has been passed down in the "Zoor Khane" Which translates to House of Strength.

Zoor Khane is a house or building going back thousands of years where warriors trained in body building, wrestling and combat arts. Zoor Khane's can be found in modern Iran.

There are a few remnants that remain from the old Persian civilization with elements of the Arab/Islamic culture mixed in after the Arabs invaded Persia and Rome in their days of decline.

Limited Ejaculation Per Male Human Life

The Chinese Taoist claim a weak man has 2,500 ejaculations in their life before they expire. An average man 5,000. A strong man 8,000, 12,000. And a superman from 12,000-25,000 Ejaculations.

That the number of ejaculations is set at birth by the amount of Qi residing in your kidneys that supply the energy of your body to create fusion in order to create and replicate new sperm.

In the movie Rocky, Micky told Rocky "Sylvester Stallone" Women weaken legs". Mike Tyson blamed his Tokyo, Japan, the fight loss on having sex prior to the fight.

I will tell you, for a male person who has not achieved Sainthood, or not a true expert at spiritual Qi Gong practice, the retention of sperm does not do much other than give a burst of energy, will do things, more insight, and generally better health.

Only one who has obtained Sainthood or is an expert disciple can use and transform the energy source that makes sperm through spiritual practice via abstinence with the help of a great enlightened Master with superpowers beyond the comprehension of modern science.

Female Masturbation Anti-Code

The female does not lose its sperm at will like the mail to weaken its life-force and life span as well as its mind and body. Rather, through their periods and the release of eggs clockwork from about the age of 13 to their late 50s.

Without a spiritual practice, attempting to achieve awaking like the Catholic Saints or a Qi Gong practice like Falun Dafa or a Taoist way, nothing can be done to increase vitality, life-span, and spiritual prowess as it connects to their vital force that is used up for sexual pleasure, reproduction or their periods.

Yes, sexual pleasure, or masturbation for a woman causes them to also reduce their life force, yet it is often inside their body and does not expel like males' sperm.

For this reason, generally, females live a bit longer because males always ejaculate and reduce their inborn Qi or life-force supply that is attached to their Kidneys and many other organs created at birth.

When the sexual supply is depleted, an organ or two begin to fail, and the human expires.

This life-force comes hand in hand with the biological clock given to you at birth, and of course there is an interdependency with illnesses you may get or how healthy you are based on your life choices.

However, if a woman masturbates, and is also losing their periods, they are doing themselves more of a disservice than men.

Because they are reducing their lifespan, health, and mental capacity by their actions as well as their periods which they have no control over unless they obtained spiritual perfection.

Chapter 6

SECRET SEX CAMERAS

Weed dealers, drug dealers, some hotel employees, spies of the rich and famous, your girlfriend, boyfriend, or someone you have casual sex with can and do without your knowledge install hidden cameras.

Sometimes it is done for blackmail, and most of the time it is done without your knowledge for the people's selfish and criminal desires.

Yes, to film someone without their permission in a private setting performing sexual acts is a criminal offense.

But, it is a gray area if you are at their home. At the very least, if you were not aware of it, it would be a civil lawsuit. I have spoken to many men who have bragged about doing this very thing. They openly brag about it to not only their friends, but strangers.

In China, a great deal of rich and famous NBA players, fortune 500 businessmen have been filmed and set up at their hotels by CCP Agents. However, other government intelligence agencies such as China, Russia, Israel and the like, have been known to engage in what is called honey traps.

For the Virginity Codes sake, if the idea of being filmed bothers you as it would most people, do not sleep around.

Because let me tell you, almost everyone lies and acts nice to get things, and that includes getting you. Find someone who will love and respect you for life. This is the key.

Sex App Engineering

Social Media Apps are designed to be addictive and to hardwire the human brain by the content viewed by the coding of the algorithms used, the electrical fields emitting from the smart phones and the interconnection of the ecosystems of Snap Chat, Twitter/X, Facebook, Instagram, Truth Social, Etc.

If the content is sexually suggestive, leading to sexual content, lewd in nature or administered by a person with sexual intentions, the user can be sexually programmed leading to infidelity, adultery, sex trafficking and prostitution.

SNAP CHAT Criminal Mind

Snap chat is a social media app with disappearing messages, images, and videos that enables criminals to traffic trugs, people and engage in prostitution.

It is simply not an innocent social media app used by millions of young kids, and Gen Z enthusiasts. Because the design hardwires the brain in a way completely unlike Apps such as Instagram, X/Twitter, Facebook, etc.

Snap Shat allows the average person, including your high school kid to be programmed with a criminal mind simply by the way the app functions and its ability to allow users to cheat on their spouses, or have hidden conduct they do not want law enforcement or the families to know.

Snap Chat is an application that is in its very design a vulnerability to the Virginity Codes relationship harmony and safety codes inside every human being.

Think about it, other than not wanting a huge thread, why would anyone want their messages and images which you can write secret messages to disappear?

In fact, the length of the thread doesn't matter when you see the last message. Hence, the main ability it offers is a way to leave secret messages and have them deleted so your family, parent, spouse or significant other do not know what you are up to.

Snap Chap fosters adultery, infidelity, drug abuse, child pornography, pornographic addiction, alcoholism, sex trafficking, human trafficking, theft, prostitution and a criminal mind even within a person who has or had no intention to commit wrong.

Now, how could the average person who has no intention of cheating on their spouse, to get into drugs, or fall into a vulnerable position like sex trafficking or cheat on a partner, simply by using Snap Chat?

How could you develop a criminal mind by using Snap Chat?

The design, program, structure and how snap chat works on the human brain and the way it allows interconnections with other mischievous personalities creates a huge eco system within the app and trains the human brain to be deceptive and to engage with deceptive people.

Your spouse may not have intended to cheat, or your kid may not have intended to meet someone and get sex trafficked, but the ecosystem of Snap Chat and its design on the human brain with disappearing messages creates these vulnerabilities on the human psyche.

The friends you may have on Snap Chat may not really have your best interest now, or at varying points in the future because the relationship developed on Snap Chat or have morphed into something toxic on Snap Chat.

Also, Snap Chat has a "Streak" Feature which attempts to get you to use Snap Chat more, and addict you more to the APP, contents and the persons you engage with by making sure you share messages everyday to reach a goal of a non-stop daily communicative streak.

Some users get so addicted that it becomes important to them and at all costs, they make sure the streaks do not end, even if the people they are streaking with are not good for them.

There is even a pay feature to get your streak back. Utterly ridiculous to have these streak features and it fosters and reduces low intelligence and an addiction that leads to all the vices as said in this Snap Chat Section as well as the porn sections.

Law enforcement and Snap Inc, the owner of Snap Chat, can at any time access your deleted messages. The user may think the messages disappear, but they never did and never do. If you think your spouse has cheated, you can use the Snap Chat app to recover previous messages.

Twitter/X

The design of X, AKA Twitter, is addicting and can program the user to be addicted to the application and its contents much like a hamster on a wheel.

The brain of the X user is hardwired to flow like the application of X and to fuse with the content the user pics to view on a general bases.

In terms of the Virginity Code, the biggest threat that exists on X is the pornography that is allowed on the platform.

The application amplifies the impact of the pornography while viewed on the platform causing more of an addiction, an additional layer of a pornographic addiction fused by a social media app designed for communication, news and education.

Instagram

Instagram hardwires the brain to watch very short clips over and over again. There are many lewd images and video clips that are detrimental to the virginity code.

Human beings and often the new generation spend hours a day watching short clips of a variety of things. From music, dance, film, fashion, animals, and a variety of different people spouting mostly short gestures and words.

The shorter a person's sentence structure is, and the shorter a clip the mind is exposed to, the easier it is to make the brain susceptible to fast and short emotion controlling stimuli and impulses on Instagram or other social media apps and platforms.

Sometimes, people who say very little and have very short sentences are very intelligent and deep, but other times, they are indicative of low frequency primal thinking and an inability to have higher thought and wisdom.

In the case of Instagram, Snap Chat, Facebook Twitter/X and the like, the short clips are making people less intelligent, less patient and more easily programmable.

Take a teenager's hormone, add a lewd video, music, and suggestive gestures, the programming already begins. The more exposure and clips they watch, the easier their brains and biochemistry get hardwired.

Later, you add a bad character, a bad influence or situation, connect it with a clip you watched that stimulated your hormones that day or a time prior, and easily you may succumb to doing something you normally would not do. Worse, if it is filmed or you are trafficked.

Hence, be aware of what your eyes and ears take in, and do not allow these people to control you with their apps, content, or lewd intentions to use you whether it is conscious, subconscious or unconscious programming from the social media accounts you view.

Facebook

Facebook is also a platform where your daughter, son, friend, or family member can be influenced, programed, or even trafficked.

It is also a communication system that is well known and gives the aura of trustability per its professional appearance. There lies one of its biggest vulnerabilities. The aura of trustability per professionalism.

People are people, and a lot of bad people act and put on an aura of goodness or purity to trick you and take advantage of you.

They use honey to get what they want rather than force as was done in ancient times with invading armies or gangsters.

Hence, trust no one is always the best motto to follow. Do not even trust yourself.

Meaning, always be assessing your own thoughts when it comes to decisions. If they come from anger, desire, emotional instability or elation, they are usually wrong decisions and or bound to get you in trouble.

DISCORD

"GEN Z" and the previous generations use discord for chats, calls, file transfers and most importantly, video game friends.

Through this application, more connections are made, and sex trafficking can occur through long-term brain washing of a young person or even an adult who is naive and in a position of need.   Video game communities use Discord often.

SEX AND VIDEO GAMES

The video game community has multiple different role playing and arena tactical games. Leage of Legends is popular as is TFT (Team Fight Tactics".

Young adolescents, especially people who have border line personality disorders, depression, bi-polar disorder, insecurities, anxiety, health problems and home life issues with parents lacking in moral virtues are hooked on these online games.

Kids in their teens and adults with issues in their 30s and 40s also use Discord to communicate, and search for friends within the gaming communities. Through the video game, the child, young adult, a female and or a male in their 20s can get dependent with a strong virtual bond to their teammates.

Sometimes, you have people in their 30s, 40s and 50s playing these games, and a part of their brain is like a child or worse. They are doing it to pray on children through the community for sex.

The more people play the video game together, the more their brains are re-hardwired not just to the game, but to their "Online Friends", to a point of wanting to meet them, having sex, and even be trafficked either forcefully or through brain washing.

The video games coding and interface allows for the human brain to re-hardwire virtually with the other players they are engaged with online.

The more they play together and build their friendships in these games, the more their brains are linked up through a digital symbiotic relationship that can allow 1 or both parties to be subject to sex and human trafficking.

Often times the human and sex trafficking are not by force, rather by suggestion and fake friendship building through the games and social media apps such as Discord, and off course Snap Chat, Facebook Twitter, Instagram and the like.

It is done via brain washing to people who are naïve, on drugs, alcoholics, in need, corrupted with mental disorders, anti-depressants or all of the above.

I played video games in my teenage years, up until probably the age of 14. I came to the realization that I was wasting my life in a fake world and building skills in a virtual fake world, rather than in our world.

I discovered that video games, albeit fun at the time, not only warp the mind, but they are destructive to the human brain, and spirit, dumbing it and weakening you.

Some even die of exhaustion during marathon game sessions. Video games can also lead to ADHD as well as being obsessed with escaping the real world, leading to drugs, alcohol, and casual sex.

Of course, a gamer, or someone that has never reached higher levels of consciousness would not feel or comprehend this very valuable perspective that is true. That video games are destructive to your body, mind and spirit as your character becomes warped.

Take for example a role-playing game such as WOW, EverQuest 2, Diablo and the like. Kids and Adults spend their valuable hours in this world upgrading a fake character, rather than their real character here that will get them closer to happiness and enlightenment.

Dating App Sex

The same vulnerabilities of sex trafficking, and trauma from casual sex exist. Especially in apps such as Tinder and the most vile of places, the fetish and swinger circles where rapists, and STDs thrive in most prevalent casual sex.

Chapter 7

Your Partners Body Count Adds to Yours.

Casual Sex Addiction

The more a person has casual sex with multiple partners, the more a part of them is lost, numb to human feelings of love.

When this happens, a dangerous state appears. The person becomes addicted to casual risky sex and gets taken advantage of.

It becomes similar to a drug, smoke or alcohol. Yet, for some, it is shameful and undignified as they get taken advantage of by many people through their addiction.

Add to it addiction to drugs and alcohol, this person, often times a girl or women, is enslavement by the 3 addictions and ruins their lives until someone, a hero, wakes them up.

At times, that hero is within you, and you simply need someone like me to write this and awaken your true self.

Parasitical Sex Addiction

Parasitical Sex Addiction will be hard for you to accept, but a few of you may think my revealing and this theory here is beyond genius.

After using certain technologies, my third eye and seeing the patterns of the micro-bacteria, I believe, the Sexual Micro-Bacteria act as a parasitical organism in order to invade, mix and multiply with other sexual microorganisms.

Hence, like a parasite, these micro-organisms send signals to your hormones, genitals, as well as your brain and other organs to become horny and stimulated for a variety of partners.

In this way, the parasite can introduce itself through you to them, or them to you. They are sexual parasites controlling the human brain as it uses the human body as a host.

Boom. This is one of the Secret of the ages revealed here as I have with many other disclosures in Virginity Code and in the public sector with the bioweapon virus lab out of China and the world lock downs all warned in 2019.

Karmic Sex Addiction and Energetic Sex Organism

Those who sleep with multiple partners, as time goes on get an addiction to one-night stands, casual sex, promiscuity and not committing because of the black energy their body absorbs from multiple sex partners as time goes by.

That black karma becomes a mass of energy requiring more black energy to sustain itself with casual sex within the multiple sex degeneracy. Because the black karmic energy is like the parasitical sex control, and organism made of energy.

The Energetic Sex Organism is like a living being made up of the negative energy acquired from each person. Their thoughts, emotions, dirt, suffering, lust, chaos, and instability all exist like a ball of matter made of energy with a thinking mind.

The thinking mind in the energetic sex organism commands the sub-conscious mind of the women or man to continue sleeping around in order for the energy to continue growing and getting knew hosts as well as dominating the original hosts body, mind and spirit as time goes on.

You can say, if the person continues down the sleeping around road, at some point, they are not only numb to love, loyalty, and the human concept of goodness, they are controlled and owned by that black karmic energy called the energetic sex organism.

The goal of the energetic sex organism is to engulf the spirit at some point. To infect the spirit and get on the spirit's body.

Humans, especially who take science as a type of religion, may not believe a spirit resides in the human body similar to electricity because there is no apparatus at the moment that can detect it available to the public. Yet, it exists.

At The AI Organization, I used my tools, my third eye, aka pineal gland and certain methods to see, detect and verify what I discovered over 20 years ago through ESP and my meditation.

I can see the human soul and even take my soul out and fly into the sky. It is similar to electricity yet looks like me and carries with it the 5 senses and beyond without needing the physical body made out of the bones, and muscles.

Human Sex Cattle Programming

Humans, People in general, are like programs born with genes and predisposition to take in information in their own unique way.

However, every single person can be programmed unconsciously, subconsciously and consciously by what they see and hear to the point where their brain chemistry, nervous system and very cells are altered by the programing.

Whether it is a friend, organization, school, teacher, therapist, parent, what you read, music you listen to and especially the videos and movies you watch, you are programmed daily and throughout your life.

Billions of people can be programmed like cattle to think, act and be a certain way without their own awareness that they were programmed positively or negatively in daily life or sexual health.

In fact, the A.I. algorithms in our social media apps, and Smart Devices allow for the most powerful form of programming known to humankind, overpowering people's free-will as if they were completely possessed.

More so, because the phones have proximity censors that emit an electrical field that connects to your electrical field altering your brain chemistry and bodily functions as you are engaging with the phone, app and being programmed by the visual or audio content you are taking in.

Religious Programming

In the past recorded 2,500 years, if you had sex out of marriage, you could be ex-communicated, beheaded, or deemed for hell.

Of-course the experiences the villages and towns had with sexually transmitted diseases that somehow became almost pandemic like during normal times and times of war where an invading army would rape the conquered town or area were passed down in history in writing, orally and by their destroyed relics.

Persia, Rome, Egypt, Greece and China have plenty of examples of historical records.

Religious programming can take an entire society to dress, think and say Pray, Lord and have a certain expected family conduct.

An entire town could be made to believe there is a witch, a demon and burn that person at the stake or excommunicate a person for not adhering to their faiths understanding.

Religious programming, therefore, had positives in keeping sexual disease and trauma at bay as long as a loving relationship was had by the husband and wife who had wed.

Hollywood Sexual Toxicity Programing

I lived in Hollywood and Beverly Hills for about 7 months on an investigation to nail the ones who were stealing my movie script AI WARS: Alien Invasion and remodifying.

During the investigation process, I also searched to see if there were ethical people there who would be interested in funding my movie AI WARS and allow me to make it for the purpose of reducing global tensions. Didn't find one that had the courage.

In the process, I met almost everyone that is "Important". So, this Hollywood section and everything else in the book Virginity Code, comes from experience, research, technology and investigation.

Opposite to Religious programming, people in Hollywood who had bad family lives with a cheating parent, a wife beater, or an unloving religious fanatic got in positions to make and produce movies, and later music starting roughly about 70 or so years ago.

And some of these producers, directors, and actors are your rapists, cheaters and those who hate to have a bonding loving relationship by way of their destructive characters and behavior.

Not all are devious, some are okay, and a lot that you may know pay other people and actresses to be their mistresses and sex toys in contracts that gives them a place to stay, drugs, alcohol, travel, shopping and involvement with film. Both contractor and the girl or boy are eventually ruined through unhealthy behavior as discussed in this book.

That being said, the people in Hollywood are multi-millionaires, 100 millionaires, and billionaires connected to other billionaires, tech oligarchs, media heads, and politicians.

Their values, or lack of, for a better word, has tainted the world and the entire family structure causing great pain, stress and suffering to all people.

Just like the religious programming provided by the humans leading the churches, Hollywood took control of what you see, hear and feel and programmed almost everyone on the planet to varying degrees to have their toxic values.

Those Hollywood haters, rapists, alcoholics, cheats, drug addicts, and intolerant sexual predators have at unconscious, subconscious and conscious levels infected the minds, thoughts, emotions, bodies, and spirits of the entire world with their alcoholism, drug addictions and sexual predator mind sets.

Their scripts, productions and movies are coded with their own sick characters that stem from alcoholism, drug addiction, instability, betrayal, pride, jealousy, power, and rape.

And when you watch Hollywood movies as you are growing up or as an adult, it is altering your brain chemistry bit by bit to become like them, and the negativity you see on TV and the movies.

This is because your eyes and ears are receptors that connect to your entire bio-electrical system. From your heart, kidneys, skin, hormones, thoughts, mind, brain, the QI that regulates your life force and even your spirit.

The sick minds and black bioelectrical energies that exist in Hollywood transfer from their movies to the audience, you.

Bit by bit, your very cells begin to change, altered, as does your brain chemistry mimicking the patterns and brain structures found in the producers, writers, actors and productions of Hollywood. Sick, twisted, depressed, deceptive, ugly and empty of virtue.

The productions that glorify violence, cheating, stealing, drugs, alcohol, casual sex, open relationships, prostitution, and the like, are infused into you. At times, it is infused into you on purpose.

Yes, the producers and writers infuse their sexual predatory frame of thoughts, drug abuse and alcoholism onto you with their movies on purpose because they had trauma growing up and hated religion or anything to do with family values.

They want to make the world like theirs, consciously. For others, it is a desire to make others like them and assimilate them to their way of being, to their world of suffering with their subconscious and unconscious minds rather than their conscious minds.

Even if you do not become like them, watching their movies, and listening to their songs, brings those frames of thought, frequencies, and their sick states of mind into your body and mind causing depression that is unseen and a disruption to your innate operating system.

You may fare well, and not be affected by much. However, your kids' beautiful mind and character can be undone in 2 hours by watching some garbage put out by Hollywood.

Yes, years of education, love and positivity input into your child's brain, can begin to be reversed and hardwired by one toxic movie put out by Hollywood.

Most of Hollywood is on drugs or addicted to some kind of substance. They are unstable people and quite depressed needing to live a life on the go.

However, Hollywood's toxicity that has led to so many broken marriages, rapes, open relationships, and diseases actually stem from the evil, stupid conduct and failures of religious community to show and display love and wisdom.

Of course, innate in humans is selfishness and irrational emotions, hence broken loves and failures in just one relationship connect and hurt an entire society through a network of cause and effect that exponentially has been multiplying.

Yes, what I am saying is, since you are part of society, a part of a family, if you hurt or fail your loved ones, you are not just hurting them, and even yourself in unseen ways, you are negatively hurting others in society through social networks.

And this social network is supported by the greatest toxic forces in history, Hollywood, social media and smart devices.

Let me reveal a big secret. Many of the Jewish producers or the men and women behind the money who oversee Hollywood, go to sleep early and get up early.

Moreover, they do not have an addiction to alcohol and drugs like the actors, actresses and production crews.

Their addiction to work, money and the perceived sense of power fades away as they get old. They are never content in their lives and never achieve true happiness.

However, as much as toxicity that has come about from Hollywood, the heroic journey and virtues of goodness has also been displayed. For good to defeat evil. For criminals who rape, kill and steal to be caught, stopped and brought to justice.

Parental SEX Qualification-

Do you think because your mom and dad had sex with each that they are qualified to be parents and raise children with a healthy mind and spirit?

The way People think of parental qualifications, especially children and society's infrastructure are absurdly optimistic.

Just because your dad and mom conceived and you came out, does not mean they are good parents, nor qualified to raise a kid. Even if they are 20-35 years older than their children. Nothing is farther from the truth.

Age does not always equate with wisdom or being a wise adult. This is true for the "uneducated", academia and Ph.D.

Level folks who read books, take exams, and write papers to get into their positions of authority.

Educated Parents lack the same qualifications as the uneducated because of the lack of virtuous qualities such as emotional, spiritual work towards perfection of one's ethical character to be good, kind, stable, strong, wise and noble.

Do your parents have bias, jealousy, greed, selfishness, toxic pride, find things offensive, intolerant, fearful, and emotionally irrational on top of being attached to alcohol, weed, medication, therapists, and the like?

If they have 1 of these qualities in excess, or more than 2-3, they are not qualified to be a parent.

What training did parents have and from who qualified your parents to raise a child and give it good values and virtues to make it strong and good in body, mind and spirit?

I will tell you, over 99 percent of parents, were never qualified to have kids, may be not even to have sex as young as they did when they had you, or their previous sexual relationships.

SEX-Qualified Mother

Just because your **mother had sex and give birth** doesn't qualify her to be a good mother, no matter how kind she was to you based on her instinctual programming to be kind.

Or maybe your mother was irresponsibly naive towards allowing you to be sexually toxic or extremely overprotective, making you sexually toxic or choosing the wrong person.

Mothers, in fact, like to control or influence their daughters and sons to be with the person they like to see or simply to mirror their mothers' degenerate values or possibly good values.

Both come from their selfishness, greed, albeit if they help you have positive values and choose the right person, it may be good for you.

Some mothers enable their daughters to be pimped or sexually promiscuous by influencing their daughters in multiple ways.

Through drugs, anti-depressants, alcohol, gifts, food, talks, threats and control. These mothers usually cheated on their previous relationship, or spouses, or were into drugs, rock and roll themselves severely altering their own brain chemistry to be failures and create a toxic family.

Of course, their lifestyle and toxicity probably were pushed or programmed into them by bad men, and more so by the Hollywood machine and music industry.

So, the blame truly can't be put all on one specific mother, even though every person has that gut feeling of what is wrong and right, what is toxic for their Children and what leads to disease.

SEX-Qualified Father

Just because your father **mated with your mother**, doesn't make him a good father. Some fathers are alcoholics, wife beaters, yell, get emotional, spend their time with their friends over their families, or simply do not have the emotional and mental wisdom to raise a human being in order to give that person virtuous values.

Yet, hurting themselves in unseen, invisible ways, as the universe has its own checks and balances beyond the comprehension of human beings, no matter how proud and intelligent they think they or what position they hold is in the human world. At the end, they are but dust.

Love Vs Age Gap

In history where civilizations consisted of books, technology and a code of morals, generally men were older than their female partner.

It was either an arranged marriage, a parent approved marriage or love. Well, the notion of love for many became something else when the feelings dissipated.

Today it is normal to see both women and men having age gaps of 20-30- years, and of course in Hollywood, even 40-50 years age gaps exist.

But what is healthy? Is the age gap healthy?

Generally, it has been said, males mature later than females when it comes to a committed relationship for life, and in some cases, it is females who mature later.

Hence, a male can be 15, 25, or even 30 years older than a female if such a male is youthful, and of great character complementing and adding to the younger partners well-being.

The same can be said for an older female. If childbirth is not to be sought because it is much more difficult for a woman to give birth to a healthy child after the age of 35-40, albeit possible.

As far as youthfulness, some people physically look, are and feel at 50 the same as others do between 20-30. And in rare cases, they not only look younger, but they are mentally young at heart.

Of course, looks are not everything, but if the older partner has had numerous relationships, and the younger has not, it probably will be a very difficult match because it really has to do with emotional and physical baggage from previous relationships.

That is more detrimental and harmful within the age gap than really the number within the age gap.

The emotional baggage from multiple sex partners, and or relationships is more toxic than the actual age. A younger person can be more experienced, and toxic compared to the older person, but generally the older, the more baggage and toxicity exists requiring someone close to your baggage.

If love is involved, then age should not matter if the parties can at least enjoy each other for 20 or more years, and relatively look close to each other in age or ableness.

Yet again, if love is involved, the toxicity from the emotional baggage of previous sex partners and or relationship will create a diminishing or interfering element in the love between two people, regardless of the age gap.

Is there a hormonal issue at play between the genders causing disputes and instability within a relationship?

They say men are generally more logical and females more emotional. I say within the men's overbearing logic exists deep hidden emotions that can make him not be a good partner regardless of age.

Within the females' emotions, exist deep hidden logic not realized because of the increased emotional state they are in mainly due to losing blood during their periods.

If a man were to lose blood and have periods, he would also be affected emotionally, and its brain chemistry altered. Both genders are in fact human.

But, they both have their limitations, positives and negatives. A man can have too much testosterone, or as the Chinese say, Yang nature. And a women can have an emotional imbalance due their periods, or in essence too much of a Yin Nature.

Hence, meditation and character building has been used throughout the ages to create balance between the genders and to harmonize their chemical imbalances, Yin and Yang Natures.

As far as age is concerned, most women are best suited to physically give birth between the ages of 20-35, albeit there are exceptions. Emotionally, it varies with age, culture, health, financial, and social circumstances.

Cyrus, you must have had 100s or 1,000s of sexual partners to obtain this knowledge about the Virginity Code?

No, I have turned down 100s of girls, and have kissed 3 girls my entire life by choice because at an early age I understood the Virginity Code and the transference of black Karma with more sexual partners and decided to attempt to reach enlightenment prior to dating.

I spent almost all my time researching, investigating and attempting to obtain spiritual perfection since my late teens and on purpose did not date until I reached 25 years of age after I reached certain levels of enlightenment that are unimaginable.

Practicing celibacy during those times, and almost all my life, and the 3 people I met you could say were not honest with me thinking I would not use my Extra Sensory perceptions, third eye, to look inside their body and see why my body is being filled up with such nasty, painful black karmic bio-electric things, that I had to eliminate through arduous spiritual practice.

My body was pure, free of any illnesses, and would not even catch a cold, and felt light and happy. So, when I mixed my body with theirs, I felt everything. But even with that, my body through years of practice and levels reached in my spiritual practice, is incredibly pure and cleaner than a newborn baby at the levels of molecules, atoms and beyond thanks to my many years of practice. In the past 22 years I never caught a cold, other than a sinus infection 1 time.

However, the average human in their lives will never feel this or the thousands of extra sensory perceptions I have come to obtain the past 2 decades. I could have blocked it out, but when you lie about these things, you can and will hurt other people in unseen ways.

Ever seen that movie with Clint East Wood 2 Mules Sister Clara? He told the Nun who claimed chastity "I never met a woman who wasn't a natural born liar" Well, for me, I would say, both men and women lie equally but use different methods, and sometimes woman who look innocent are the most diabolical liars.

Now, I am totally against those men who sleep around and try to get an innocent woman with a low to zero body count.

Here, I am only describing the relationship with body counts as described in this book Virginity Code and how it brings upon your illnesses, sadness and emotional trauma the more you have and the more you engage in risky promiscuous casual sex.

More importantly, the added karmic bio-electric fields form various partners makes enlightenment and happiness even more difficult.

And my taste and standards were too high. Could never find a pretty girl of high ethics with spiritual quality that I was attracted to, who had zero or very low numbers in her past making up her health, mind and spirit today.

You really must find a match with a person whose energy compliments yours or matches yours. And that has a lot to do not just by the way the two are made up upon birth, but how many partners they each had alters their brain chemistry, mind, body, values, health, and spirit as well as the energy inside their body and consciousness.

Thus, choose wisely whether you are a man or a woman, consider the virginity code, the information I wrote here about how your mind and health are affected by your partners.

If you are in need of Q and A, you can attempt to reach me on a live for Questions, or better yet, book a personal session with questions in hand by contacting me through email or social media.

I would like to tell you, the reader, something very important.

In 2019, after 1000s of hours of investigation, I predicted, detected and warned orally and in writing that a mutating replicating bioweapon or virus from China would be launched, causing enslavement, death, mandated vaccines with nanotechnology, riots, loss of democracy, censorship with AI, global hypersonic nuclear wars and a technocratic tyranny ensuing in the later years. This was detected and seen in detail with my third eye and verified with my intel teams globally.

I notified the Secret Service, Directors of intelligence Agencies, Fmr. CIA Covert Ops Director, the Presidents close advisors and friends, ran global press releases that were turned down in Oct 2019, published books in 2019, and global federal documents in Dec 2019 and Feb 2020 that reached over 2 billion people via Twitter and other social media platforms.

About 300 podcasts had me on, and I was able to spook the pentagon during lockdown with my UFO film Documentary called AI The Plan to Invade Humanity that got the pentagon to release and admit that we have had off world spaceships land here and there were aliens inside.

And my twitter request to the President to declassify our UFO files was put into the covid bill and I was on Coast-to-Coast, a prominent UFO show with George Noory , a total of 6 times.

Now, in terms of your lives, your family and how you suffered.

Every major media outlet and major podcaster was notified of the lab by me. Wallstreet Journal reporters were following me and my company on Twitter, and many of the Presidents Generals and Admirals were not only reading my documents and books but had me on shows as did Hollywood elites and heavy weight champs.

However, all of the major media outlet owners, CEOs sent global notices to their editors to not allow their reporters to run my story that your lives were in danger not just from the bioweapon, but from lockdowns, loss of jobs, and mandated nano-tech vaccines that I coded in my disclosures showing it causes heart and birth issues for some and I specifically stated that the vaccine would not stop transmission.

I was offered over 100 million dollars for contracts by the conservative side as well as the liberal sides, but they all required me to not have total freedom of speech and I did not want to be against half the nation for ethical and spiritual reasons during the pandemic, even though I was in no way close to wealthy, rather like the average person as I never sought money nor fame. I focused instead on spiritual perfection for 2 decades.

After some book sales, as a CEO, I only had about 50k in savings, and turned all the money down because I knew if I didn't write my documents, and get on the shows, and do the social media posts, a lot more people would have died globally, and you and your families would have suffered greatly.   In fact, if you do your research, you will see the information I put out saved the lives and freedoms of many people globally.

A great deal of podcasters, twitter accounts, and famous people watched me and rephrased what I revealed globally, getting the word out, yet hurting the world because they plagiarized and were not competent. They hurt themselves as well, because the universe has a code for cheaters, and it sets them straight in time.

The thing is, it was a cat and mouse game. The conservative elites were afraid masses of people will find out they didn't listen and my intel warning about the lab in China was stolen for money.

And the Liberal Elites were afraid masses of people will also find out and their names, power and money would be at stake.

So, behind the scenes, they worked with podcasters and big twitter accounts to watch everything I put out meant to save your lives and freedoms, and censor, delay and take it for their own platforms for their books sales, fake power and so on. Not realizing, the universe is watching them.

There were times I'd have 100k people follow me in one day, and almost everyone would fall off. I did a Tweet called "Subpoena This" which had many of the pentagon Generals Retweeting, even though my account was shadow banned. It reached over 180 nations, as did my documents via other social media accounts.

It had to do with the sex tapes, and the Islands of girls being trafficked. It became global as well, and again I saw from my friends copies of notices from media outlets stating "Do not run his story or his name"

And the podcasters and "patriots" who claimed censorship, actually were in on it as well. They hid everything I put out about AI, the Bioweapon, Mandated Vaccines, and lockdowns by using religion for their own fame. It didn't' help that I am a mix of Persian, Germanic, Greek about 75 percent, 17 percent Chinese, and I believe may be some black and Jewish at 8 percent.

So as a mixed looking person, it was hard to be supported. But there were other supernatural reasons why. As the future cannot be told in detail. The Universe has a code, if you see it in detail, it is forbidden to tell the people in the program who are oblivious to it and have not achieved enlightenment or levels of it.

Let me tell you, in the year 2003 I had what they call an awakening, and strengthened my third eye that was open since a child and many extra sensory powers, so I could see the future of the planet to some degree as well as our universe.

In 2008, I had higher awakenings, with over 10,000 energy circuits opening in my body and allowing my brain to compute millions of thoughts in seconds with my current spiritual practice started in the year 2002.

I could see and scan people's thoughts globally, and had developed many martial arts abilities through my practice.

I saw exactly how the virus was being built, I told President Trumps French director Mickael Damelincourt at the Trump

Hotel in Washington DC and the Secret Service in June 2019 that within 6 months the bioweapon from China would arrive and told them right before the election it would hit the President. He had the personal cell phone to Ivanka, Don Jr, Eric Trump, was in contact with Pres. Trump regularly and was merely half a mile from the White House.

It was even published in my 2019 book Artificial Intelligent Dangers to Humanity on pages 252-253 with some coded language that I gave that report to a Trump contact in D.C.

I even explained to Mickael, who is French and was very close to the President and the family, how the bioweapon would flow into the White House undetected and people would not know they had it, and so many other things. I predicted 1000s of things like that with clockwork precision.

So, you may ask what is my qualification to write this book. I can tell you I have a Bachelors Degree in International Security and Conflict Resolution, a Masters Degree in Homeland Security, three years in a Ph.D. program, secret intel work and advisory to the CIA Covert Ops Director, lived with fighting monks in China, and have trained under my Master here in the U.S for almost 20 years.

And the power and teaching I got from my teacher, which developed my third eye, wisdom and other abilities, were all used to reach over 3 billion people during the pandemic behind the scenes.

With all of that, I sacrificed greatly, and financially need support. Thus, the way you can support me back is to donate to me and to my companies so I can make AI WARS: Alien Invasion and cover my overhead. You can also buy the books in bulk, tell others too and request advisory sessions for your personal lives and business by booking private conversations with me.

However, know this, do not ask me to see your fortune or future. Rather, the advisory will be based on wisdom and what is the best ethically right path for you to take to better your situation in accordance with the universe.

Thank You for listening and reading.
Cyrus A. Parsa
The AI Organization and God Studios

Twitter/X   @Cyrusaparsa1   @aiorganization

Instagram   @Cyrusaparsa1

Email Consult@theaiorganization.com
Contact@godstudios.com

Book Cover Image Credit Dreamstime.com

www.ingramcontent.com/pod-product-compliance
Lightning Source LLC
Chambersburg PA
CBHW062107080426
42734CB00012B/2786